295. C

Cover:
The Château
Pages 6/7:
The King's Bedchamber

Printed and bounded in Italy
by S.T.I.G.E. - Turin

VERSAILLES

Its history, its splendor and its gardens

MOLIÈRE

collection
SPLENDEURS

VÜE PARTICULIERE DE LA CHÂPELLE
Prise du Coté

DU CHATEAU DE VERSAILLES.
de la Cour.

CONTENTS

VERSAILLES AND ITS HISTORY

A bit of history

Detail of the Marble Courtyard

The buildings surrounding the courtyard, paved with black and white marble, still have the brick façades and slate roof of the first Louis XIII edifice. Louis XIV, who was loathe to destroy the heart of the original castle, instructed Le Vau and Mansart to adorn the walls with busts, columns and ironwork in keeping with the new constructions. The Roman busts featured on the façade recall the important influence of Antiquity on 18th century art.

From a small country chateau to the symbol of French influence over the entire 18th century, it seems that Versailles was destined to be built against all odds. The palace is the result not only of royal fiat; it also reflects the evolution of the arts, ideas and mores at the turning point when the 17th century age of faith shifted to the 18th century age of enlightenment. In this sense, Versailles offers a great lesson in history. It reveals the particular tastes, engraved in stone, of each of the sovereigns who lived there from 1630 to the Revolution. It also bears the traces of a retinue of artists, architects, gardeners, courtiers and anonymous figures who generated the taste and climate of the times, still visible in the painted ceilings and the paths of the castle gardens. "The mind completes its own thoughts by expressing them," said Louis XIV in his *Memoirs for the Instruction of the Dauphin.*

Versailles is undoubtedly the result of this same alchemy. The King became increasingly carried away with the work, and it soon became a constant source of concern.

French kings have always enjoyed hunting, but perhaps none as much as the hotheaded Henri IV. He took Louis XIII hunting for the first time when he was only six years old, near the Chateau of Saint-Germain, "in the vicinity of the windmill on the way to Versailles," recounts his physician, Héroard. Louis XIII may have lacked his father's petulance, but he inherited his passion for the hunt and passed it on to his own son. In 1623, young Louis XIII had a pavilion built on the site of the mill, where he would spent the night after protracted hunting parties.

The edifice was built on what was still a modest estate of "forests and water". Set on a hilltop, it overlooked a small church dedicated to Saint Julien (where the Hôtel des Postes now stands) and the old castle of the Gondi family, who had followed Marie de Medicis to France. The décor was plain: plaster fireplaces, tile floors, and tapestries on the walls of the four rooms reserved for the King. No accommodations were planned for the queen, or indeed for any women other than the caretaker's wife. Here, Louis tolerated the presence of a few faithful friends, with whom he could relax and play billiards, backgammon, *la renarde* or chess. Soon, he was spending more and more time at Versailles. He made an exception to the rule in 1626, when he receive his wife, Anne of Austria, and his mother, Marie de Medicis, though they did not stay overnight. It was the first festive occasion at Versailles.

Louis quickly grew attached to the land, well away from the cliques and boisterousness of the Court. In 1630, on the Day of the Dupes, he called Richelieu to Versailles to consolidate his authority in the face of the Queen Mother. In 1632, the King finally acquired the seigniories of Versailles and the Gondi coat of arms was replaced by the three fleurs-de-lys of the Crown on the elmtree gibbet. Louis XIII then enlarged the park and surrounded it with a wall, and asked the architect Philibert Le Roy to furnish and embellish the house. The "Little House of Cards," as Saint-Simon described it, came into being, made of brick, stone and slate. The royal apartments took up the first floor of the twenty-six-room construction, which was protected by a moat in the medieval defensive tradition.

The chateau in 1722

This painting by Pierre-Denis Martin admirably illustrates everyday life at Versailles, both in the courtyards and the palace environs. Pictorial representations of the castle offer precious testimony to the myriad transformations it underwent over a period of many years. Here, we see the fence separating the Court of Honor from the Royal Courtyard, which was destroyed during the Revolution. Louis-Philippe had an equestrian statue of Louis XIV erected on the same spot.

The heart of Versailles was now definitively established. Louis XIV never touched the core of the castle despite the huge waves of remodeling that followed. His successors, whether for sentimental or budgetary reasons, also respected this choice.

When Louis XIII died, Anne of Austria and her two sons were forced to wander, balloted by political unrest. Louis XIV, who was born in Saint-Germain, was thirteen years old when he first discovered Versailles in 1651. Ten years later, at the death of Mazarin, the King took possession of "his" castle at the same time he came to power. It was the beginning of a fifty-four-year personal reign, dedicated to glorifying both his power and his palace. After the troubled years of La Fronde, Louis was determined to turn the castle into a symbol of his royal grandeur and of France's supremacy. Fouquet was

the one who awakened the King's passion, in spite of himself. The famous scene took place on August 17, 1661.

Young Louis XIV had often heard about the superb castle his Superintendent had fitted out with splendid taste and luxury. He asked to be invited and, by royal fiat, set the date for his own reception.

The residence was perfectly habitable and Fouquet's numerous guests, including the celebrated La Fontaine, had already vaunted its charms. Yet the Superintendent, who was given barely a month's notice, was absolutely determined to receive his sovereign with as much pomp as possible. He decided to offer a sumptuous feast, enlivened by the sparkle of fountains, fireworks and spectacles that would remain forever engraved in the memory of the guests.

Never did a glorious plan backfire so badly. It was already a challenge to organize such an extravaganza in a still unfinished residence, but Fouquet nevertheless achieved the impossible. His wish to dazzle the King, however, proved a terrible blunder. Anne of Austria's austere Louvre and the little chateau of Versailles were light years behind the refinements introduced by the Superintendent. The feast on August 17, 1661 was indeed superb, but it was Fouquet's undoing. From that very day, the young King decided to ruin the Superintendent who had accomplished such an extraordinary feat in honor of his coming. Colbert, who loathed Fouquet, was instrumental in the Superintendent's downfall.

Louis XIV decided that such luxury could only have come from funds embezzled at his expense, and he immediately had Fouquet arrested and his possessions confiscated.

Our purpose here is not to study Vaux-le-Vicomte, but it seems fair to assert that, without Vaux-le-Vicomte, Versailles would never have existed and that Fouquet's extraordinary wealth was, first and foremost, the result of playing his role properly. The King had asked Fouquet to find new sources of credit, and had put him in charge of state revenues. Fouquet himself had often used his own property to secure loans for the King and his personal success was a sufficient guarantee for those who trusted him.

Fouquet was arrested by the famous musketeer, d'Artagnan, and at the trial, the King made a virtually unheard-of request to have the punishment increased. The master of Vaux-le-Vicomte spent the rest of his life imprisoned in the Fortress of Pignerol.

Louis XIV immediately engaged the artists of Vaux-le-Vicomte in the task of transforming his father's castle. The three men who gave Versailles its essential features – Le Nôtre (1613-1700) for the landscaping, Le Brun (1619-1690) for the decoration and Le Vau (1612-1670) for the architecture – were already the most renowned of their time. The artist's name was used to sign the work of everyone in his workshop. Nerval talks of "those modest men (who) submitted to a great intellect, more eager to achieve immortality for their works than for their names." All of Versailles expresses this diversity blended into a single design.

Although monarchs traditionally considered themselves patrons of the arts and letters, this role was

as much a pleasure as a duty for Louis XIV. His mother, aided by Mazarin, an experienced collector, shared her love of art with him. Louis also learned a great deal about architecture during his travels and achieved an elegant synthesis at Versailles, before the rest of Europe began copying his style. His influence was felt well beyond the 18th century, as two hundred years later, Ludwig II of Bavaria was clearly inspired by Versailles, especially in designing his Herrrenchiemsee castle.

Versailles was gradually transformed from a mere overnight dwelling into a privileged residence. Contrary to tradition, the castle had permanent furniture, well before the Court was officially established there. "His Majesty wished all the apartments of the those to whom he had given them be furnished. He fed everyone and even provided firewood and candles (…)," reported Colbert.

Louis XIV, by Houasse

Louis XIV on horseback, Louis XIV in his armor. Louis XIV ordering the construction of the Academy and the Observatory. Louis XIV at the siege of Douai. The representations of the Sun King are as numerous as they are varied. It was useful, moreover, to remind the people that the King was not only the consummate aesthete of Versailles, but also a sovereign capable of showing interest in the sciences and of leading troops to war in defense of the country's interests.

The Yew Ball

The marriage of a dauphin was anything but a love story, even if the spouses happened to find each other attractive. Its primary purpose was to seek out diplomatic alliances, and in passing, an occasion to give new commissions to the craftsmen who gravitated around the Court. This ball was organized to celebrate the wedding of the son of Louis XV, the dauphin, to Maria Teresa, the daughter of the King of Spain, who died the following year, leaving behind her an inconsolable widower. There was another inconsolable widower was at their wedding ball on February 25, 1745. It was King XIV, who was mourning the death of his latest mistress, the Duchess of Châteauroux. Among the events planned at the masked ball was the arrival of unusually clipped yew trees, one of which served as a disguise for the King himself. Everyone knew that the King's heart was ready for the taking, and a splendid young woman succeeded in so doing. Born Jeanne-Antoinette Poisson, she had married a nobleman named Le Normant d'Etioles. She is known to posterity under another, more famous name: Madame de Pompadour.

The chateau was perched on a narrow hill, surrounded by marshes. Colossal earthworks were undertaken to enlarge the gardens. At first, the King's resolute determination to "force nature" did not please Colbert, the new Superintendent of Finance. Worried about the heavy expense and Louis XIV's lack of interest in the Louvre, he did not hesitate to write to his sovereign in 1664 regarding Versailles: "This house has more to do with Your Majesty's pleasure and entertainment than with your glory."

When Louis XIV contemplated adding wings onto the original chateau in 1665, Colbert was again critical: "All that one can hope to do is patch up something that will never be fine. Beautiful houses must be elevated (…) whereas Versailles is almost hidden from the lower ornamental pond by the tiered flowerbeds… To anyone with a taste for architecture, the castle will look like a small man with large arms and a big head, in other words, a monster of a building (…)."

Once Colbert was appointed Superintendent of Building, Arts and Manufacture in 1664, and then General Treasurer Controller in 1665, he overcame his reticence and expertly orchestrated the works.

The artistic disciplines, which he organized with care, proved to be a solid asset for French prestige and trade in Colbert's struggle against imports. He had the marble quarries in the Pyrénées opened up again after centuries of abandon. In 1662, he created the Manufacture Royale des Gobelins to make furniture and tapestries, under the direction of Le Brun until 1690, followed by Mignard and Robert de Cotte. Shortly after his death, the French Manufacture Royale des Glaces was built in Saint-Gobain in 1685 to produce mirrors. All of these places were genuine laboratories, allowing French artists to develop a new style.

In the same spirit of supervision, copyrights were initiated in 1689, requiring booksellers, printers and engravers to register their works under pain of confiscation.

During the construction works, Louis XIV was quick to show his admiration for the artists in his service and his generosity towards them knew no bounds. Despite the Sun King's majesty, he did not take offense one day when Le Nôtre, enraptured at the sight of his own landscape artistry, literally hugged him with joy.

The King made daily visits to the works, showing an astonishing attention to detail. Whenever he was away from Versailles, his correspondence with Colbert was filled with questions and suggestions. He worried as much about the width of the fountains as about the wall covering of his suite, and enjoined his Minister to hasten the pace of work. Everyone had to submit models, samples and plans, which he annotated and modified, making final decisions on everything only after taking time to listen to other points of view.

Though Versailles was conceived as a political manifesto, the King's passion soon became mixed with reasons of state. He was so eager to hear admiration expressed for his new domain that he held his first great feast in 1664 in what was still a huge work site. Until 1666, Versailles remained a place for celebrations, after which guests returned to Paris or slept in their carriages. The idea of making it a palace to live in, as well as the seat of government, was beginning to form in the King's mind.

In 1668, Le Vau produced an Italian-style "envelope" for the façade giving onto the gardens and the two wings that extended the Marble Courtyard. After his death, Jules Hardouin-Mansart took control of the buildings, expanding them still further, in accordance with the King's wishes. For thirty years, Jules Hardouin-Mansart remodeled the chateau, until it finally looked much as it does today.

To create more housing space, he erected the Ministers' wings in the style of Louis XIII on either side of the Front Courtyard.

Next pages:
The Marble Courtyard
La Fontaine's writing not only featured talking animals, he also personified the Marble Courtyard speaking from within an immortalized Versailles:

"I consider myself content and I embrace my destiny.
For the bedchamber in which the King rests
Is so close to my ground
That his balcony juts out into it.
And when day breaks,
And the hero takes the morning air,
I am fortunate to be the first thing
He sees through his eyeshade."

The three windows on the balcony bring light into the king's bedchamber, in the center of the palace.

Next, two large, recessed north and south wings were added onto the main section, in keeping with the Italian-style "envelope" on the garden side, whereas the center of the castle, previously taken up by a terrace, was adorned with the sumptuous Hall of Mirrors.

At the same time, the Petites and Grandes Ecuries (stables) were built on the Parade Grounds. The small stables housed the draft horses and coaches, while the large one offered 820 feet of mangers for riding horses. Finally, as Le Vau's Orangery had disappeared when the castle was extended, a new one was built, flanked by two monumental Stairways of the Hundred Steps. J. Hardoin-Mansart spent the last years of his life launching the construction of the Grand Trianon and the current chapel.

During the same period, in 1671, the King decided to have his estate extended by a town. "His Majesty, having the town of Versailles under his special protection, wishes to make it as flourishing and well-frequented as possible (...)." Louis XIV granted exceptional tax advantages to all those who decided to build in his town, and even made it impossible for their property to be seized. The town offered considerable advantages for noblemen required to invest heavily in clothes, horses and carriages as well as servants in order to maintain their standing at the Court, thereby weighing dangerously on their often precarious resources.

By the death of Louis XIV, the chateau looked roughly as it does today, at least from the outside. Jacques Ange Gabriel added the Opera, a marvel of modernity in 1770. The only part of the major remodeling project actually built was a small neo-classical wing with a pediment and a colonnade, erected to the right of the Entrance Court. All the other modifications at the time concerned interior fittings. At the end of his reign, Louis XV added a Petite Trianon to the Grand Trianon, which would later be especially favored by Marie Antoinette. Finally, the Hamlet was built for her, surrounded by a garden designed in the newly fashionable "English" style.

Emperor Napoleon did not like these places and rarely went to the Grand Trianon. Furthermore, he closed the French School museum set up in the apartments that were deserted at the time of the Revolution and used them for a time to house old soldiers of the Guard.

Oddly enough, it was Napoleon, the "Citizen-King", who undertook the restoration of Versailles, which he had completed at great cost and paid for in large part from his own estate. In 1833, he decided to dedicate the castle "to all the glories of France." Four years later, Louis-Philippe inaugurated the historical museum with a banquet for six hundred people. All the political and artistic celebrities of the time came out from Paris for the great occasion: Hugo, Dumas, Musset; Balzac, Vigny and Saint-Beuve crowded into the Hall of Mirrors.

The guests were first entertained by performances of Gluck and Molière, and then were invited to admire the art works on display, lit up by five hundred and fifty torchbearers.

Unfortunately, the newly organized display rooms replaced the ground floor apartments and much of the decoration of the former palace. On the other hand, the museum had a salutary effect in preventing the palace as a whole from falling into what was already a worrying state of deterioration.

Versailles, emptied of its occupants and its furniture by the Revolution, suffered damage to its buildings and grounds. Chateaubriand described "those statues, those fountains, those woods... now all covered with moss." Louis-Philippe at least succeeded in avoiding the total ruin of this cumbersome inheritance, which had been neglected until he took over.

During the war of 1870, the Prussians moved into the chateau, while leaving the museum open to the public. When Bismarck and his officers attended the crowing of Emperor Wilhelm in 1971, the Hall of Mirrors was again used to host the event. Once Versailles became the seat of the National Assembly, it enjoyed the life of a garrison town. It was only in the 20th century, through the efforts of Pierre de Nolhac, and all the chateau curators who came after him, that the furniture and décor from the time of the Kings was gradually restored, piece-by-piece. Today, thanks to the efforts of historians, artists and craftsmen over the years, we have a clear picture of how the Court lived for a hundred years and of the development of the arts during the same period. In each of the restored rooms, we can step into a moment in the lives of 17th and 18th century Frenchmen, and leaf through another page of French history.

Life at the Court

"A sovereign goes against his duty when he dissipates the substance of his subjects (...). But perhaps he does still greater harm when, through inappropriate frugality, he refuses to spend money on that which serves the glory of his nation." Twenty years after the first works were completed, when Louis XIV had achieved the desired décor for "the glory of the nation", he made Versailles the official residence of the Court, which succeeded in drawing the envious gaze of neighboring countries and gave new meaning to the notion of monarchy.

A note in Mercure de France on May 6, 1682 indicated that the Court was now established at Versailles. The King and his entourage had always moved around a great deal. Servants, attendant merchants and "furniture" followed the Court as it went from the Palace of the Cité to Vincennes, from Fontainbleau to Chinon, and from the Louvre to Saint-Germain-en-Laye. During their peregrinations, the courtiers led a relatively free existence until François I decided to regulate their attributions. When Henri IV became king, strict Court habits were again relaxed. As the first Bourbon to be crowned, Henri had not enjoyed a royal childhood and he preferred to surround himself with companions rather than vassals. Good King Henry lived with his friends in a more family-like atmosphere than his predecessors.

For his grandson Louis XIV, on the other hand, etiquette was the very foundation and expression of power. "Those who think that these are only ceremonial affairs are greatly mistaken. As the peoples over whom we reign are incapable of grasping what is essential, they ordinarily regulate their judgments by what they see on the outside." Etiquette was also a powerful tool to guarantee the obedience of the particular group who had threatened royal authority during La Fronde, namely, the nobility. Court etiquette henceforth determined everyone's rights and duties, and every moment of the day was scheduled in an immutable order. Throughout his reign, Louis XIV endeavored to strengthen his hold over the nobility, and even to counter them by encouraging the establishment of a few families of the Grande Bourgeoisie. The sovereign gave out honors and privileges as well as high military and ecclesiastical positions to the nobility, but they were denied a political role.

Detail of the Fountain of Animals

To keep the Court at Versailles and ensure there would be no more outbursts like La Fronde, nothing was too majestic to remind everyone where the real power lay. The lion, along with the sun, was one of the most explicit symbols.

Louis XIV as a child

The childhood of Louis XIV was austere, marked by the unrest of La Fronde. The splendors of Versailles were first and foremost a reaction to the rigors and lack of prestige associated with the Louvre, a fortress situated in the heart of Paris, which he had fled precipitously during the night of January 5-6, 1649, when he was eleven years old.

The decision-makers, who also depended on the King's good will for their positions, were bourgeois. When Saint-Simon again expressed his resentment against the "long reign of the vile bourgeoisie", a sentiment no doubt shared by many of his peers, he was thinking of Louvois, Colbert and Le Tellier.

The social organization reigning at the Court mirrored the concentric architecture radiating around the royal apartments. Louis XIV considered himself the foremost servant of the State, and as such, forced himself to observe the rules he dictated.

When the castle was finally populated, the multitude of people surrounding the royal family were carefully ordered and housed according to their rank. With each marriage, death and disgrace, the occupants of Versailles saw their apartments shifted or modified to reflect their new status. First came the princes of royal blood, such as Condé or Conti, the King's cousins, then the dukes and peers whose numbers swelled under Louis XIV, followed by the counts and marquis. Only dukes could be made peers and thereby gain access to the Parliament. This prerogative kept them apart from the rest of the nobility, with or without titles, who formed more or less rival factions, depending on the source of their rank (purchase of land, ennobling responsibilities, a favor of the King, etc.).

Those who held important responsibilities (Head Chaplain, Head Equerry, Head Chamberlain, etc.) were also housed in the chateau and its outbuildings.

Palace duties were organized on a quarterly basis, with a different head for each quarter, adding up to a total of one hundred household officers, along with musicians, painters, sculptors and miscellaneous artists that the King wished to have at his disposal at all times. The organization of the Queen's apartments was modeled on that of the King. Finally, the corridors were filled with armies of domestics, made up of men without property. While it is difficult to calculate with any exactitude, the resident population of the chateau at the time of Louis XIV may be estimated at about three thousand people. For exceptional occasions, such as weddings or births, the figure might triple, and Versailles became a hive of activity. Such abrupt population growth was accompanied by memorable traffic jams. During the century of Louis XV, on the eve of the wedding of the Dauphin, in 1747, it took carriages three houses to travel from Paris to the castle.

Indeed, the roads were hard to negotiate, bogged down in mud in wintertime, and rutted year-round by wagons loaded with materials, animal herds and hay carts, in addition to travelers' teams of horses.

However burdensome its etiquette may have been, life at the Court was not as ethereal as one might think. "I wish you could see the Court," wrote Primi Visconti, "it is an utter chaos of men and women (…) a mixture of people, a continual rustling (…)." Even after the reign of Louis XIV had ended, the courtiers were still living on a construction site teeming with workers. On a single day in 1685, a count was taken showing thirty-six thousand workers, toiling in the buildings and gardens. The courtyards were used as workshops where materials were piled up, whereas the walls of the town-side of the castle were lined with small stands selling souvenirs, refreshments or food.

In the courtyards and the vicinity of the palace, mixed in among the merchants and scribes paid for their writing skills by workers far from home, were ladies of doubtful virtue who sold their charms quite illegally.

According to an actor at the Hôtel de Bourgogne, the courtiers of Versailles were "chameleons and tablecloth mowers, eager to know which way the wind is blowing." They lived in a sumptuous, noisy setting, with one, single, overriding concern: to please the King and obtain a higher position. La Bruyère (who died at Versailles) wrote mockingly: "Those who live in this land have a philosophy that is not candid, as they are all tangled up in a mass of foreign hair." People fought to obtain a garret at the chateau or a cubbyhole in the vicinity. Until the reign of Louis XV, when families built their own town houses built, salvation lay exclusively inside the castle walls.

Louis XIV strove to see his Court entertained, as he wanted them to be present in great numbers and splendidly dressed. At the first great feast at Versailles in 1664, called "Pleasures of the Enchanted Island," he gathered together about six hundred guests. The Court did not stay on for extended periods until ten years later, when for the first time the King decided to spend the entire summer at his new palace in 1678. The courtiers had trouble keeping up with the lifestyle imposed by the Court. Most of their revenues came from distant estates, which they could only rarely visit, since everything at Versailles depended on remaining within the King's gaze, and the benefits that reached them often vanished en route to the palace. That explains why courtiers showed such zeal in seeking the slightest responsibility carrying a recompense or advantage in kind.

Everything was a possible source of profit in the "huge seraglio," as Balzac described Versailles. Used candles, household linens and the outfits of the royal family, as well as leftovers from the table were distributed in accordance with strict rules, which brooked no exception without creating a scandal. Far from a mild activity, this trade represented a significant income for its beneficiaries. The privileged ones, who had direct relations with the King, did not hesitate to make money from their position. Mademoiselle de La Vallière herself agreed to present a petition to him so long as she was paid for her efforts. It was also possible to be rewarded for denouncing, or even imagining, a case of embezzlement. Intrigue, in all its forms, was propagated as a source of gain.

The nagging lack of money gave rise to feverish enthusiasm for gambling among the courtiers, who could pay off all their debts or be ruined completely in a single day. There was also a craze for lotteries, which had been in fashion since the beginning of the 17th century. One of the most famous lotteries, held in 1681, had a huge prize attached to it, which was won by the King, as he had bought an enormous numbers of tickets. Louis XIV was elegant enough to put his winnings back into play.

Versailles retained a medieval flavor, in that the sovereign was not cut off from his subjects. The gardens, the castle corridors and a large portion of the royal apartments were open to the public. To maintain some sort of order amid the tumult, the military household, under the authority of the Constable, fortunately had numerous men available: the Royal Bodyguard, the French Guard, the Gardes de la manche, and the famous Swiss Guard.

Dressed in Renaissance-style outfits, wearing velvet hats with white feathers and slashed sleeves and holding halberds, the Swiss Guard surrounded the throne during ceremonies and the royal coach whenever the King went on a journey. The French Guard wore blue uniforms with red facing and high golden collars.

Along with the Swiss Guard, the French Guard was the most prestigious corps. Whenever the King left the palace or returned, they formed a guard of honor stretching from the doorstep to the gates of the courtyard. The twenty-four Gardes de la manche never left the King's side, exchanging their swords for halberds and their jerkins for coats of mail when they escorted him to the chapel. Some fifty Gate Guards, under the direction of a captain, oversaw the security of the chateau during the day, their swords and rifles at their sides. At night, the Swiss Guard and the Royal Bodyguard took their place. The latter were key elements in ensuring the safety of the King who selected them himself from among his horsemen. Under Louis XV, they were given a their own town house.

Louis XV as a child

The two sovereigns who left their mark on Versailles were not raised there. Louis XV was taken away from the castle at the age of five upon the death of his great-grandfather, Louis XIV, in 1715. He did not return until the year of his coronation at Reims, when he was twelve years old and engaged to the daughter of the King of Spain, whom he did not wed in the end. Early on, the notions of grandeur and majesty inherent in his future role as sovereign were inculcated in him by his partisans, who represented the interests of the Bourbons against those of the Regent, Philippe d'Orléans.

Finally, the Military Police Guard, under the Grand Provost Marshall of France, made up a sort of police force parallel to that of the bailiff: these forerunners of today's French policemen were only allowed to carry clubs. Skirmishes between the various groups were not infrequent, even though they were theoretically present to maintain order. A concern for precedence and etiquette also prevailed among the guards, which did not facilitate their coordination or efficiency. One day the King asked to have the doors of a drawing room closed, and it took three quarters of an hour before the proper attendant could be found and the order carried out.

Theft was commonplace in the confusion of the comings and goings. Outdoors, gardeners continually

accompanied the King on hunting expeditions, bringing the dogs to him and gathering the game. A hall was provided for them in the stables, where their off-duty mischief occasionally went too far, but they were usually treated indulgently because of their youth. No punishment was meted out to the unfortunate page that nearly set fire to the monarch's wig one day with a swerve of his torch.

The *Service de la Bouche* or food service also contained an enormous reservoir of people. The kitchens originally installed in the castle itself soon took up so much space that the Court had barely arrived before J. Hardouin-Mansart had to build the Grand Commons to house them, cramming valets and ushers into rooms that were often the size of a closet.

The Mansart Gates

The six monumental gates are the pioneering accomplishments of what is now known as corporate sponsorship. In 1856, the ironwork factories of Edgar Brandt offer to recast for the French government the gates designed by Mansart and Delobel, which were destroyed during the French Revolution. The work was carried out using 18th-century techniques. Brandt had not yet begun manufacturing household appliances.

replanted the flowerbeds, from which visitors immediately picked bouquets, and the copses had to be protected by a fence to save them from constant ravaging. Anyone caught in the act was put in the stocks.

In addition to the turbulent soldiers, a group of about one hundred and fifty pages brought a touch of youth to the palace and the town that is often mentioned in literature. The young men (age fifteen to eighteen) were recruited from noble families of long standing. They had to be five feet five inches tall, an imposing height for the time. They spent their mornings learning about weaponry and riding as well as dancing, and the rest of their time in the stables or in the King's Chamber. Some attended the King's rising and retiring ceremonies, carried torches when he moved about the palace, and served buffet meals in the Royal Apartments. Others

Today the Commons is as a military hospital, located on Rue de l'Indépendence américaine.

Feeding the Versailles population required an impressive procurement system and there was an enormous amount of waste, in spite of supply contracts and inspections by the bailiff. The staff that served at table were entitled to the leftovers. They soon overstepped this privilege, and instead of leftovers, whole shipments of food were being sold in the vicinity of the castle. There was no dearth of buyers, as the town boasted a hundred inns at the end of the 17th century. Sumptuous lodgings, used to house habitués of the palace for whom there was not enough room and prestigious travelers, stood cheek-by-jowl with eating places offering crowded quarters for workers and visitors from far and wide who had come to admire the Sun King's chateau.

Apollo

Opinions are divided regarding the symbolic meaning and identification of the sun and its god with the Sun King. Some people believe that the designation actually dates back to ancient times. One thing is certain: everything at Versailles tended to identify Louis XIV with Apollo, the god of light. The brilliance of the statues and sculpture groupings serve as a constant reminder that one is in the domain of a powerful master.

In 1696, an edict was issued prohibiting pigs from roaming the streets, although until that date (at least), inns located even a few meters away from the supreme luxury of the palace were surrounded by vegetable patches and small animal farms.

In addition to cabaret owners and their customers, the town soon attracted tailors, linen makers and milliners, since one could not appear at the Court without a cascade of ribbons and trinkets. When Molière depicted the excesses of "precious" courtiers, he was only mildly exaggerating. Canes, which came into fashion at the time, were more than mere accessories; they helped keep one's balance despite the flourish of ribbons adorning shoes and heavy wigs. Ladies' hairdos became infinitely extravagant. First came the *Hurluberlu* style, then the *Fontanges*. The latter, a scaffolding of lace-covered wire, sometimes equipped with a device to flatten the entire hairdo in order to get through doors without a collision, was more the work of a locksmith than of a wigmaker.

Alternating periods of war and peace influenced the waves of construction work, and one could read the political and economic situation of the moment in the clothes worn at Versailles.

The Gates of Versailles

These gates are no doubt one of the symbols most frequently used to represent the wealth of France's artistic heritage. The coat of arms of France atop this splendid piece of ironwork recalls the fact that we owe many of the masterpieces that have given France its international reputation today to the kings of the Old Regime.

In his final wishes, Louis XIV expressed a desire to see his successor, then five years old, raised in a healthier place, for the immediate vicinity of the chateau still contained marshlands. His nephew, the Regent, took young Louis XV to Vincennes and then to the Tuileries in Paris in 1715. Versailles dozed for seven years until June 1722, when Louis XV returned to the palace at the age of twelve. No doubt the young King had pleasant memories of Versailles, but the decision seems to have been made for reasons of state. After Law's Louisiana investment scheme went bankrupt, the country and its sovereign were caught up in a delicate game of alliances and they had to find a way of reasserting their authority. Returning to Versailles did just that.

Louis XIV was in the habit of punctuating the year with trips to Marly or Saint-Germain, but Louis XV increased the number of sojourns away from Versailles. In some years, he spent less than six months there.

While Louis XV perpetuated the traditions established by his great-grandfather, he also stretched the rules to set the tone for the new age. The heaviness weighing upon the Court in the final years of the reign of Louis XIV dissipated in the 18th century. Every night the King decided on the time for the waking ceremony the next day. Worse still, in the eyes of traditionalists, before returning to his bedchamber for the morning ceremonies, the King indulged in escapades that took him to Paris, where he frequented the Opera and went to balls. Sometimes, he even received his ministers in the apartment of Madame de Pompadour, who was far from enjoying the semi-official status of Madame de Maintenon.

Under Louis XV, private life took on hitherto unknown importance, although it never encroached on the King's functions. His Public Dinners still took place, but he had a summer dining room set up under the eaves for "little suppers". Such moments, when the sovereign amused himself in pleasant company by making and serving coffee like an ordinary bourgeois, were reminiscent of the "elegant suppers" held by the Regent at Palais Royal. The courtiers appeared to follow the King's example by detaching themselves from their castle apartments, which they henceforth kept only for official receptions. They often acquired town houses near the castle or in Paris. Imperceptibly, the structured world over which Louis XIV had ruled began to disintegrate. With lampoons, songs and nicknames, the Court began to take unheard-of liberties, as the gap between the various leagues grew wider.

Amid this tumult, the Queen, Marie Lezsczynska, seemed the epitome of good behavior. She is shown playing a hurdy-gurdy and the clavichord, and painting under the direction of Oudry, La Fontaine's famous illustrator. She devoted her afternoons to visiting convents (she founded the order of the Dames Augustines de Versailles), and when her husband was dining out, she spent the evening with the Duc and Duchesse de Luynes. Marie died in 1768, as discreetly as she had lived. That same year, Madame du Barry took the place of Madame de Pompadour in the King's fancy. Once again, the King chose a favorite who was not of noble birth, thereby creating conflict.

When the Archiduchesse Marie-Antoinette arrived in Versailles to wed the Dauphin in 1770, instant rivalry sprang up between the two women, and through them, two new clans clashed at the Court. At the death of the King four years later, Madame du Barry was immediately exiled to her estate in Rueil.

Then came the reign of Marie-Antoinette, whose fresh spontaneity combined with already shaken Court etiquette could not fail to arouse hostile feelings. For the first time in Versailles, the Queen dared to break away from customs she considered old-fashioned and develop a new style of living more to her liking. She received her hairdresser, the faithful Léonard, who was to follow her in the journey to Varennes, and her official dresser, Rose Bertin, unceremoniously and at great length. Similarly, she put an end to the tradition prohibiting any man from serving her directly. Finally, she invited guests to her table without concern for precedence, according to her fancy.

She was soon held responsible for the King's financial worries. Her contemporaries condemned her for spending fortunes on adornment, as well as for scorning convention. Marie-Antoinette introduced familiarity into the life of the Court which was reinforced by the cheerful behavior of Louis XIV. The King, who was curious about

new inventions, fascinated by the voyages and discoveries of his time and who spoke kindly to everyone, was thought to be lacking in majesty by the "old-timers". Whispering filled the hallways, and the palace was increasingly deserted as soon as compulsory ceremonies were over.

The Queen, who escaped from the chateau to the Trianon or her Hamlet, surrounded by only a few companions, increased the resentment of all those who were excluded. Even her brother, Joseph II, judged her severely: "She does not follow any etiquette (…) which would be fine for a private individual, but she is not doing her job (…)." In this tumultuous atmosphere, Versailles received an outstanding visitor in 1778: Benjamin Franklin came to ask for the French government's help, two years after the Declaration of Independence of the United States. In 1783, the first experimental balloon flight took place. The Court was experiencing the beginning of a new world, as the former one began falling apart.

On May 4, 1789, a procession from the Church of Notre-Dame to the Cathedral Saint-Louis brought the representatives of the three orders, behind the King and Queen, to mark the opening of the Estates General. The crowds that came to see the last great spectacle at Versailles were no longer there for merrymaking and rumblings of hostility were mounting.

On July 14, the first emigrants went into exile.On September 23, Louis XVI, who had been fearful since the General Estates, added the Flanders regiment to his guards. A heavy atmosphere weighed upon the castle and the town, as the mobarchy lived out its last moments. The winter was harsh and famine struck the countryside. At the same time, the absence of wealthy families already in exile created hardships for those who depended on them for their livelihood. A little over a hundred years after Louis XIV established his power at the chateau, Louis XIV and the royal family left Versailles on October 6, 1789.

Detail of the Trianon peristyle

In 1687, J.H.-Mansart replaced Le Vau's fragile Porcelain Trianon by a marble Trianon. Built to offer an escape from the constraints of castle protocol, it nevertheless housed the Court's most illustrious members: the Queen, the King and his mistress of the moment. Another side of Court life flourished at the Trianon, where the King enjoyed a private existence, even serving coffee himself. Yet Versailles was made for receptions, and splendid feasts were often held at the Trianon, far from the boring palace residents.

THE CHATEAU

The architecture

Of all the edifices in France, Versailles may well be the one in which the desire for symbols reached its peak. There are two key notions serving as principles on which everything is based, like the parts of a theorem: first, the notion of a perfect neoclassical style, and secondly, that the style has no purpose other than to enhance the glory of the Sun King.

The sober initial architectural lines were constantly heightened by important accessories such as gilding, paintings, the natural landscape and even the stone of the statues. In the gardens, the illusion is simple but undeniable: Apollo, the god of the sun, is resplendent in a myriad of allegories. As soon Louis XIV came to power, he decided to make Versailles the most perfect expression possible of absolute monarchy. The task of the architects was to materialize this desire. The end result was superb.

Along with the Louvre colonnade, Versailles symbolizes the high point of French neoclassicism, resulting from the work of Le Brun, who was supported by Colbert, during the second half of the 17th century. Indeed, in 1663, Le Brun, who was unanimously acknowledged by the Royal Academy of Painting and Sculpture, put forth a set of theories, which he presented in a lecture series.

Later on, in 1671, when the Royal Academy of Architecture was founded, Blondel also played the role of theoretician, expounding ideas inspired, for the most part, from architectural traditions dating back to antiquity. For Le Brun, whose unquestionable masters were Raphael and Poussin, the essential traits of neoclassicism can be summarized in a few words: the strict use of straight lines

at right angles and regular curves where required; compliance with mathematical proportions and symmetry; the adoption of a fundamental model on which the entire construction is based; sober construction; a prohibition against mixing different architectural orders on the same storey.

Indeed, it meant a return to ancient architectural ideals, with their requirements of sobriety, consistency and harmony in an attempt to achieve, as far as possible, perfection.

The splendor of Versailles comes from the scale on which all the artistic domains are combined, without ever getting in each other's way or detracting from each other: painting, sculpture and architecture form a unity of outstanding quality that has rarely been equaled in the centuries that followed. Many sovereigns in the 18th century considered Versailles the perfect reflection of absolute power and adopted it as a model.

The Chateau of Versailles grew out of a small hunting pavilion built by order of Louis XIII between 1624 and 1638. In fact, there were two different edifices: the first was destroyed and was replaced by a little castle with a moat, built by Philibert Le Roy in a purely French tradition, combining brick, stone and slate. For a number of reasons, Louis XIV decided to preserve the original core building, which is situated today at the very heart of Versailles, around the Marble Courtyard.

As early as 1661, Louis XIV had already decided to make Versailles his royal residence, and he undertook all the works required to achieve this transformation.

Projecting sections, trophies and emblems

This partial view of the façade is a true lesson in architecture. On the ground floor and the first floor, a section of the building projects out to enliven the façade. On the second floor, the attic has been given especially elaborate treatment. All along the balustrade, trophies alternate with fire holders (the name comes from the shape, which looks like a cresset). The entablature is surmounted by emblems and pilasters. On the first floor, a niche appears between the two projecting sections. On the ground floor, the French doors are surmounted by mascarons; the stones of the wall are rusticated.

There were three main phases in the construction of the chateau and its outbuildings, ending in a sort of microcosm of gardens and buildings radiating out of an ideological center, the Royal Apartments, thereby strengthening the desire for centralization so dear to Versailles.

From 1661 to 1666, Louis XIV ordered the famous Le Vau to carry out the first changes in the pavilion of Louis XIII, which he completely modified by adding gilded gates, marble colonnades and busts inspired by antiquity. At the entrance to the castle, he built the Grand Commons equipped with kitchens and stables to house courtiers when feasts were held at Versailles. Unfortunately, there is nothing left of the original Orangery built in the gardens. The first modifications of the gardens were sketched out by Le Nôtre in line with the main axis of the Tapis Vert (green carpet) and the Grand Canal.

occasions ever organized by Louis XIV, the Marble Courtyard, the original entrance to the castle of Louis XIII, received its definitive décor on the three projecting sections made of stone and brick. On the central façade, Le Vau (and J. Harduoin-Mansart for the upper sections), added eight small marble colonnades on the ground floor, topped by a finely wrought iron balcony made by Delobel. The façades were also adorned with eighty-four marble busts, placed on brackets and balustrades, adorned with large vases and located at the meeting point of the walls and the roof. At the King's request, the courtyard itself was paved with black and white marble to prevent coaches from driving by in front of the Royal Apartments.

From 1666 until 1683, Versailles underwent a series of radical transformations. The ongoing incentive for these works was to enlarge the palace, which was destined to replace the Louvre and become the new royal

Aerial view

The 18th century never imagined that one day Versailles would be seen from the sky yet, from this angle, the domain is a credit to its builders. Elegantly closed on the eastern side by the two horseshoe-shaped stables, the main section of the building is lengthened by two slender wings, which fit naturally into the play of ornamental parterres (the South Parterre, the North Parterre), and extend to the Water Parterre and then the Parterre of Latona.

Nearby, a small, pleasant pavilion was built called the Menagerie. Dedicated to scientific pursuits, it once preserved rare animal specimens but it, too, has vanished. The three main avenues leading up to the Parade Ground of the chateau also date from this same period: the avenues of Sceaux, Paris and Saint-Cloud. Slowly, and under increasing control, Versailles and its décor came into being, tending towards every greater glorification of the Sun King.

In May 1664, on the occasion of the "Pleasures of the Enchanted Island", one of the greatest festive

residence. Louis XIV originally intended to replace the main section built by Louis XIII, but in the end, he decided that this core should be preserved. The old castle was then "wrapped" on the garden side in an "envelope" made up of three buildings in keeping with the initial U-shaped plan. On the north and south sides, the new projecting sections were slightly recessed in relation to the original construction, thereby creating two small inner courtyards near the Royal Apartments. The new façades facing the gardens were designed by Le Vau and continued by François d'Orbay after 1670, drawing their inspiration from Italian villas.

Built of stone, they included a rusticated ground floor, decorated with large arched windows, a storey with Ionic columns and, on the top, an attic with a balustrade roof. The entire façade was decorated with numerous sculptures above the projecting sections.

Alongside these exterior additions, Le Brun, at the head of a multitude of painters, artists and sculptors, began decorating the Royal Apartments with incomparably splendid gold, marble and paintings. In the southern section, a marble staircase was added, leading to the Queen's Apartment, which was remodeled in the 18th century; in the northern section, the famous Ambassador's Staircase led to the King's quarters.

Starting in 1678, J. Hardouin-Mansart, appointed head architect by the King three years earlier, took over the direction of the construction work at Versailles. The building plan grew to astonishing proportions with the addition of the north and south wings

on the right and left. Built by Mansart in 1679, they doubled the castle on either side, but the long suite of apartments intended to house royalty and important officers was profoundly changed in the 19th century.

On the town side, the grandeur of the buildings, which still had their façades of stone and brick, seemed to be diminished by the recess of the Marble Courtyard. On the garden side, on the contrary, the view was admirable, a long vista punctuated by regular arched windows.

The writings of Count Alexandre de Laborde describe the view with great precision: "This is the spot where one must stand in order to judge the grandeur of this unusual palace; from here, it can be seen in all its beauty, surrounded on one side by vast courtyards to which truly royal avenues lead, and on the other side, by gardens that have become legendary for their magnificence and ornamentation."

The French Pavilion

Gabriel designed this little pavilion for Madame de Pompadour and Louis XV. Erected in 1750 in the French Garden, adjacent to the New Menagerie, it was used as a stopping place by the sovereign when he came to visit the animals on his estate.

"The architecture is elegant and rich. On a base with a hundred and twenty-six openings stand Ionic columns forming the first storey, which supports a Corinthian attic and a balustrade decorated with trophies. This façade, or rather these three façades, measuring eighteen hundred hundred feet, together have a hundred and twenty-five casement windows on the first and second stories, which form three hundred and seventy-five openings onto the garden (…). The three sections, at first detached from each other, were reunited to form the largest and most monotonous façade ever seen."

Indeed, J. Hardouin-Mansart believed he could cheer up the façade by adding peristyles or loggias, each one bearing as many statues as it had columns. Similarly, in 1678, at the request of Louis XIV, Mansart came up with the idea for the famous Hall of Mirrors on the former terrace site designed by Le Vau. Facing the garden, it is situated on the "noble" floor of the central building and joins the southern and northern sections over a length of 73 meters. To complete the splendid palace complex, Mansart had two magnificent stables erected at the Parade Ground, on either side of the Avenue de Paris, which were finished in 1685. The even proportions and the choice of adornment made them remarkable edifices, each one comprising two wings flanked by two small pavilions attached to the main part of the building by a curved section, with an arching shape that adds further grace to the whole building.

Thus stood the Chateau of Versailles in 1682 when Louis XIV decided to make it the official residence of his Court and a new Royal Palace. The huge constructions, subdivided on the interior, were used to house the royal family, their guards and ministers and the families that formed the sovereign's entourage.

Alexandre de Laborde summed up quite well the effect produced by Versailles when the construction work was finally completed: "At the sight of these prodigious buildings, one was no longer tempted to criticize their faults. The long line of the façade, uninterrupted by pavilions or any other protruding building that would have masked its grandeur, had a look that was unique in the world, and one could not even find its likeness in the ancient world. Although erected at different times, the palace seems to have been conceived and built in a single stroke. Some say it is an unworthy parvenu, that it is the body of a bird with disproportionate wings; but such thoughts were incapable of troubling the effect this splendid, gigantic monument had upon one."

Sunburst emblem

On either side of the entrance gates, the lyre of Apollo surmounted by a sunburst emblem surrounded by superb fleurs-de-lys, evoke without a doubt the domain of the Sun King.

The last construction phase at Versailles began in 1683 and continued until 1715. J. Hardouin-Mansart not only completed the works already under way, but with the help of Robert de Cotte, he built the large Orangery, which is located in the South Parterre and considered one of the most beautiful pieces of architecture in the world. When it was finished in 1685, it offered a spectacular view of the gardens of Versailles. The last experiment involved building the Grand Trianon, a sort of pleasure pavilion in addition to the main residence. This was the condition of Versailles when Louis XIV died in 1715. The Dauphin, then five years old, left the oversized palace until he reached adulthood, and Versailles fell into neglect for a few years. When Louis XV finally returned, his aim was not to expand the palace, like his predecessor, Louis XIV, but to make it more pleasant to live in.

He sacrificed the Ambassador's Staircase to build the Small Apartments, subdividing the rooms as far as possible into boudoirs and small studies. Jacques Ange Gabriel, the King's First Architect, proposed a complete remodeling of Versailles, aimed at altering the town-side façade to give greater privacy to the Marble Courtyard and the Louis XIII core building. The death of Louis XV put an end to the works,

however, though only one wing had been built. Despite the King's appalling financial situation, Gabriel succeeded in completing the theater, drawing his inspiration from the Olympic Theatre in Vicence, built by Palladio.

Under Louis XVI, the only addition was the Hamlet of Marie Antoinette's Petit Trianon, designed by Richard Mique in a perfectly charming style. The neoclassicism introduced in the décor marks the last stylistic experiment at Versailles.

The Revolution brought a period of mourning upon the palace of the Kings of France, and the chateau only narrowly escaped ruin through the efforts of Napoleon.

There is a note of bitterness in the musings of a traveler visiting Versailles after 1789: "Here was once the seat of a powerful empire; these places, now deserted, were once enlivened by a multitude of people; the walls, where gloomy: silence now reigns, rang out with cries of joy and festivity, and now, here is all that remains of such far-reaching domination: a gloomy skeleton, a dark, vain memory, the solitude of death; the palace of the kings has become a den of wild animals! How could such glory be eclipsed?"

The French coat of arms

Overlooking the main gate, the fleurs-de-lys and royal crown indicate from afar the mark of the Bourbons. The fleurs-de-lys are surrounded by Apollo's laurels.

The interiors

The ground floor

Since Versailles was designed to be a dazzling manifestation of royal power, it was to be expected that the grandiose décor of the interiors should be unrivalled, even by foreign Courts.

The first floor lent itself admirably to Royal Apartments, with windows giving onto a view extending all the way to the horizon, in accordance with the wishes of Louis XIV. To emphasize the majesty of the place and set the tone, there was nothing quite like a gigantic staircase. That is how the prestigious Ambassador's Staircase came into being in 1672, for it had not been part of the original building plan.

When Louis XIV first brought his family to Versailles, it was relatively small. When Madame de Montespan was to be housed at the castle, however, an almost "bourgeois" problem of living space arose.

The Sun King decided to remodel the interior, moving the chapel onto the side of his wife's apartment, thereby gaining extra room for Madame de Montespan. From then on, the ground floor was repeatedly rearranged.

Madame de Montespan, born Françoise-Athénaïs de Rochechouart de Mortemart, was the King's favorite. She naturally enjoyed being surrounded by luxury and works of art, and her contemporaries reported marvelling at her apartment situated on the royal floor. Louis XIV soon enlarged his personal domain by turning a section of the ground floor into a very luxurious Bath Apartment, a magnificent suite reserved for the relaxation of the King and his mistress. He even had a secret staircase connected to this apartment, which was removed when Madame de Montespan fell from favor due to a murky affair related to poison. She lived on at Versailles for a few years as a recluse on the ground floor, before leaving the castle in 1691. There is nothing left of her apartment today.

La Palatine and her husband, Philippe d'Orléans, brother of Louis XIV, and later their son, the famous Regent, lived on this floor. Next, it was occupied by Louis XV and the ten children he had with Marie Leszczynska, though no accommodations seem to have been planned

The Hocquetons Room

This splendid room, a triumph of trompe l'œil artistry, was the room from which Louis XIV most frequently when out into the gardens. The Hocquetons Room, adjoining Madame Adélaïde's Great Cabinet, opened out onto the palace grounds and was the hall of the Ambassador's Staircase

for her. The décor of Versailles is filled with sculpted and painted images of children, though few were actually raised there. When they were not in line for the throne, they were put in the care of nannies outside the castle.

It became clear that all of the daughters of Louis XV could not all stay at the chateau (seven out of Marie Leszczynska's eight daughters survived, along with one of her two sons). Adélaïde, the most resourceful, who could get anything she wanted from her father, was allowed to remain, along with her two elder sisters, Elizabeth and Henriette. The others were sent to Fontevrand, where one of them died shortly afterwards. Victoire, Sophie and Louise did not return to Versailles until they reached adulthood in 1748 and 1750. The Duchess of Ventadour, who had already raised Louis XV, was the governess of the three little princesses living at the palace. The girls spent their time, like their brother, playing games, visiting the animals at the Menagerie and studying the history of France, classical languages, English and Italian. Artistic subjects, including drawing, painting, singing and music, played a large role in their education. The boy showed a predilection for singing, and was often accompanied by his sisters on the harpsichord or the violin.

Later on, the Dauphin lived with his wife in other rooms of the main section, which have since been restored. The rooms contain beautiful examples of wood panelling with raised turquoise decorations and overdoors featuring seascapes by Vernet.

Although living space was scarce, Louis XV nevertheless accommodated Madame de Pompadour on the same floor, where she stayed until her death. Madame Adélaïde and Madame Victoire lived in separate apartments on the ground floor until the Revolution. Nattier painted numerous portraits of them, which are now on display, representing them as the goddesses Diana or Flora. A particularly splendid overdoor can be found in Madame Adélaïde's room.

Another dauphin couple, Louis and Marie-Antoinette and their three children, also lived here from 1782 to 1789. Later on, in the 19th century, the ground floor of the main section was completely remodelled into gallery rooms. Pierre de Nolhac took the initiative to restore these rooms in the early 20th century. Today the restoration is at least partially completed, after years of research and major works projects.

Four apartments have been restored: those of the Dauphin, the son of Louis XV and of his second wife, the Dauphine Marie-Josèphe de Saxe (mother of Louis XVI) on the south side, and those of Madame Victoire and Madame Adélaïde on the north side.

The north wing

When Louis-Philippe set about restoring Versailles, he commissioned huge historical frescoes from the greatest painters of his time. The 16th and 17th century galleries containing paintings of the reign of Louis XIII and the early reign of the Sun King are located between the Opera and the Chapel, on the site of the former apartments of the Duc de Maine (the legitimized son of Louis XIV and Madame de Montespan) and the Bourbon-Conti family.

The Crusades Room stands opposite, featuring a set of paintings commissioned by Louis-Philippe. With its coffered ceiling, it is a superb example of the neo-Gothic style in fashion at the time.

The south wing

Louis-Philippe converted the first floor into a splendid museum of Napoleonic history. By asking one of the most renowned artists of the age to represent the epic tale of the Consulate and the Empire, Louis-Philippe sought to reconcile disappointed revolutionaries, frustrated Bonapartists, the Republic and its constitution and the royalists with the restoration of Versailles.

In contrast to the first floor, the ground floor presents a delightful aspect of royal life in the 18th century. It was a suite of apartments used as living accommodations, dominated by two complementary elements: white walls heightened everywhere by piers and beautiful paintings, forming a visual museum of the 18th century.

The Dauphin's library

Recently restored, this room is an admirable example of the rococo style of the 18th century. The son of Louis XV liked to withdraw to this study, adjacent to the apartment of the Dauphine, his beloved mother Marie-Josèphe de Saxe.

The first floor

The salon of Hercules

Later on, Louis XV had the Salon of Hercules added on to the State Apartments and the Ambassadors' Staircase removed.

Under Louis XIV, this room was the upper part of the fourth chapel. It was transformed by Robert de Cotte, and then by Jacques-Ange Gabriel when the current chapel was built in 1712. Work was interrupted when the King died in 1715, and did not resume until ten years later. The walls are covered with polychrome marble, heightened by twenty red marble pilasters with gilt bronze bases and Corinthian capitals. The marble and bronze, together with the dimensions and sober lines of the room make it one of the most imposing in the entire palace.

The room is named for the large cornice with military motifs that encircles the ceiling called *The Apotheosis of Hercules* by Lemoyne. The 1,033-square-foot painting was done over a single expanse, rather than divided into compartments. The work proved fatal to the artist, who, in utter exhaustion, took his own life shortly after its completion.

The gigantic composition, painted from 1733 to 1736, earned him the title of the King's First Painter. Lemoyne represented a profusion of characters, including Jupiter, Venus, Neptune, Apollo, Morpheus, etc. Hercules is surrounded by Cupids and Graces and is being feted by all the gods of Olympus. In all, the nine groups in the painting contain one hundred and forty figures.

The room, which was intended for receptions, also boasts two paintings by Veronese: *Eleazer and Rebecca*, above a chimneypiece carved by Antoine Vassé and, covering the entire opposite wall, *The Repast at the House of Simon the Pharisee*. Louis XIV, who was especially fond of Italian painters, had received the two paintings from the Republic of Venice in 1664. After a sojourn at the Louvre, *The Repast* was taken to Versailles in 1730.

The Salon of Venus

The Ambassador's Staircase formerly led to this room, known as the Marble Room, and to the Salon of Diana that follows it, known as the Billiard Room. Here, in the marble niche, stands a statue by Jean Warin representing Louis XIV as a warrior in ancient times.

In 1777, this prestigious room was transformed into a Throne Room in honor of the ambassadors of the Bey of Tunis. On May 2, 1789, Louis XVI received the delegates from the National Assembly here before the opening of the Estates General. At the reception, each of the three orders wore their respective official dress, offering one of the last spectacles of the kind before the fall of the monarchy.

The State Apartments

The suite of six salons, known as the State Apartment, was decorated between 1671 and 1681, and has come down to us more or less in its original condition, a rare occurrence at Versailles. This explains why these rooms exhibit similar decorative inspiration, corresponding to the early Louis XIV style.

"Since the sun is the King's emblem, we have taken the seven planets as the subject of the paintings for the rooms comprising these apartments," explained Félibien. In addition to the mythological themes, the rooms as a whole show a certain unity in the materials used, the treatment of the richly painted ceilings and the sober lines of the wall decorations.

At the time, the State Apartments were reached by the Ambassador's Staircase, which was unfortunately destroyed during the remodelling undertaken by Louis XV, with two ramps leading up to the Salon of Venus and the Salon of Diana.

Here the King provided entertainment for his Court every Monday, Wednesday and Thursday of October until the beginning of Lent. The events, known as *Soirs d'Appartement*, were synonymous at Versailles with recreation. Yet, here again, there was no room for improvisation.

The King decided on the hours (7-10 p.m.) as well as how his guests would occupy themselves. Louis XIV was eager to have the members of his family take part in these evenings. "Madame, I wish to hold an *Appartement* and for you to dance at it. We are not like private individuals. We owe ourselves completely to the public," he told the Dauphine.

The Salon of Abundance

This was where the courtiers took refreshment during *Soirs d'Appartement*. Louis XIV had made it into the "royal game room" where, the *Mercure Galant* tells us, "the entire Royal Household descends from its grandeur to play with members of the assembly who have never been so honored."

The ceiling by René-Antoine Houasse (1644-1710), a disciple of Le Brun, who often contributed to the décor of Versailles, represents an allegory of *Royal Magnificence* surrounded by cupids in the center, whereas the edges are adorned with painted gold vases and bowls. One overdoor is done in gold monochrome, repeating the theme of Abundance, the perfect name for a room containing some of collections of Louis XIV.

The King had a lifelong fascination with rare objects, stones, paintings, books and sculptures, which he liked to put on view in his showcase-chateau. In 1681, he had a room fitted out to display the most prestigious items called the Cabinet of Medals and Curiosities. The gilding, brocade, mirrors, garlands and trophies on the walls were an ornate setting for the silver and gold objects, jade and jewels shown in small cabinets in a series of niches. Some of the pieces from this collection are now at the Louvre.

The Salon of Abundance, which led to the Medals Cabinet, was naturally permeated by some of its refinement and splendor. In 1955, the green and gold velvet tapestries were repaired and hung on the walls as they had in the 17th century. Today, the room holds portraits of the children and grandchildren of Louis XIV by Rigaud and Van Loo. Four busts of patinated bronze, on either side of the door, recall the King's taste for characters from antiquity. Finally, the Boulle-style medal cabinets, made by his contemporary, Oppenordt, reveal the art of Versailles furniture. Introduced amid a profusion of marble wall panels and dazzling fabrics, a piece of furniture had to be given sumptuous, polychrome decoration. Marquetry developed rapidly and André-Charles Boulle, though not its inventor, was one of the craftsmen most skilled in this technique.

All remodelling took place under the watchful eye of Le Brun until 1683. He designed the motifs for wall hangings and silver furniture himself, and his ornamental style, reminiscent of embroidered gardens, even influenced the work of cabinetmakers. Precious wood was inlaid with ivory, copper, mother-of-pearl and gilt bronze and carved, turning furniture into full-fledged works of art.

In this room, Madame de Pompadour sometime performed on a movable stage. One day, she presented *L'Enfant prodigue* in the presence of Voltaire, the author, recently returned from exile.

The Salon of Venus

One must try and imagine tables brimming with delicacies and pyramids of fruit put out to tempt food-loving courtiers between dances or card games.

On grand occasions, eight candelabra and silver chandeliers lit up the two trompe l'oeil paintings by Jacques Rousseau, opening up perspectives that give this room a special charm. Statues, also in trompe l'oeil by the same artist, alternate with the windows.

The ceiling, by René-Antoine Houasse, is divided into compartments richly decorated with gilded, sculpted stucco, like the cornice along the edges. The central motif gives its name to the room: *Venus, crowned by the Graces*, unfurls flower garlands that bind the feet of Bacchus, Vulcan, Mars, Neptune and Jupiter.

Mythological couples adorn the corners, including Jason and Medea, Theseus and Ariadne, Titus and Bernice and Cesar and Cleopatra. In the coving, events from the early reign of Louis XIV such as the Carrousel of 1662, the works undertaken at the King's chateaux, his wedding and the War of Devolution of 1667 are echoed in episodes from antiquity.

The rear wall contains a niche with a full-size statue of Louis XIV as a young man, wearing Roman military dress.

The Salon of Diana

Louis XIV, a great lover of billiards and an experienced player, used to come here to enjoy a few hours of freedom. La Palatine did not share his interest in the game, which she described with severity: "We go to the billiard room, and everyone bends over and no one says a word to anyone else." The King played tirelessly on a table covered with crimson velvet and fringed in gold, while the ladies looked on from raised platforms set up around the room and covered with Persian rugs.

Since 1975, the room has been decorated with eight marble and porphyry busts standing on plinths, which, for some of them, means a return to their original location. Marble covered the walls adorned by Louis XIV with trophies and gilt bronze cupids where he displayed a bust carved by Bernini in 1685.

This white marble bust reveals the Italian's sculptor's superb technique: the draping, the hair and the facial expression illustrate the dynamic quality Bernini gave to stone. The artist had made the sculpture twenty years earlier, when he was at his peak (he was sixty-seven) which filled the subject, a twenty-seven-year-old King, with admiration. The famous Italian consented to come to France only after lengthy negotiations. Yet, during the five years he spent going back and forth between Paris and Versailles, Bernini, known familiarly as "The Horseman," showed little enthusiasm for French art works, and hence, despite his genius, he was regarded rather unsympathetically by a number of French artists.

Even Bernini's talent was not always convincing, and his projects for remodelling the Louvre were rejected. They were refused for several reasons. No doubt economic reasons played a part, as well as the King's growing passion for Versailles and waning interest in the Louvre. Moreover, the baroque style was far from the sober classicism fashionable among French architects at the time. A further fiasco occurred when an equestrian statue of the King arrived at Versailles in 1685, which Bernini, who had died five years earlier, had made upon the request of Colbert.

The statue so displeased the King that he had it modified by Girardon, and then relegated near the Fountain of Apollo, and finally exiled to the far end of the Swiss Pond. The statue (or at least a lead reproduction of it) now stands on the esplanade of the Louvre. In spite of everything, Bernini's work is present today at the other stronghold of the monarchy.

The overdoors are treated in monochrome, each one reproducing a theme from the cult of Diana: Blanchard represented *Diana and Acteon*, *Diana protecting Arethus*, *An Offering of Flowers* and *A Sacrifice to the Goddess Diana*. Above the mantelpiece hangs a painting by Charles de Lafosse, showing *Iphigenia kidnapped by Diana as she is about to be sacrificed*, and on the opposite wall, *Diana forgetting her former resolution never to love, comes to find Endymion*, also by Gabriel Blanchard.

The Salon of Mars

A portrait of Marie Leszczynska in the rear, and The Family of Darius *to the left of the fireplace, have returned to their original places which indicates, in contrast to the preceding room, that the visitor has entered the King's Apartments.*

The Salon of Mars

Within the walls of this game room, the gambling fever at the castle seems to have reached a peak at the *Soirs d'Appartement*. During all the reigns, the Court was passionately involved in playing, and as games of chance were prohibited in Paris under Louis XIV, they were all the more appreciated at Versailles. Princess Palatine recounts: "One player would yell, another would bang on the table with his fist so loudly that everyone in the room could hear. A third cursed to make one's hair stand on end." The often enormous amounts of money that were wagered account for such unexpected scenes in this setting, adorned with magnificent silver furniture until 1689. Many a dispirited courtier had to leave the room, utterly, ruined.

The Salon of Mars was originally a guardroom, a fact to which its military decoration still attests. Three painters worked together on the ceiling: Audran for the central motif, *Mars in his Chariot pulled by Wolves,* Jouvenet for *Victory borne aloft by Hercules,* and Houasse for *Terror and Fear invading the Powers of the Earth.* They filled the covings with large monochrome medallions presenting themes from antiquity.

On either side of the chimney, two raised platforms were set up for the *Soirs d'Appartment* where the musicians were seated. Platforms were introduced in 1684 by Louis XIV, shortly after the Court was finally established at Versailles, but Louis XV had them removed in 1750. As a result, the room was transformed into a sumptuous ballroom and concert hall. The huge rug covering the floor, which was produced by the Manufacture de la Savonnerie, once adorned the Louvre Gallery in the 17th century.

The paintings hung on the red damask wall covering are all worthy of mention: *The Walk to Emmaus* d'après Veronese, the portrait of Marie Leszczynska in full Court regalia by Vann Loo, and that of her husband by the same painter; *The Family of Darius at the feet of Alexander* by Charles Le Brun; finally, over the mantelpiece, *David Playing the Harp* by Louis Dominiquin, which Louis XIV had selected for his bedchamber.

The Salon of Mercury

The damask-covered walls were once adorned with magnificent paintings by Titien, which are now hanging in the Louvre. The only piece of furniture back in its original place in the room, which was once used for ceremonies by Louis XIV, is the famous Morand clock, a gift to the King in 1706. Through the glazed panels on all sides, one can admire the clockwork, which sets the automatons in motion.

The Salon of Mercury

When his grandson was proclaimed King of Spain in November 1700, Louis XIV gave him this room, which had been his antechamber, and then his own ceremonial room), until Philippe V regained his throne in December. A few months later, he was to sleep there himself, while awaiting the completion of work on his new bedchamber giving onto the Marble Courtyard.

Prior to 1689, this room contained the royal bed, one of the greatest of the many luxuries that abounded in the King's State Apartments, which was placed behind a baluster made out of a ton of silver at the Manufacture des Gobelins by the goldsmiths Loir and Villers.

The baluster, like all the pieces made of gold or silver found at Versailles, was melted down in support of the War of the League of Augsburg. When Louis XIV died, his body was laid out on the first day in the bedchamber of the Marble Courtyard and then brought here the following day. For one week, from September 2 to September 10, 1715, seventy-two priests said Mass, relaying each other from dawn to midday at four altars set up in the room for the occasion.

The ceiling, with its abundant gilded cupids and festoons, is the work of Jean-Baptiste de Champaigne. The motif in the center bears a particularly interesting name: *Mercury in his chariot pulled by two roosters, preceded by the Morning Star and accompanied by the Arts and Sciences.* The covings were used for scenes from antiquity, while the gracefully painted angles are inlaid with gold monochrome medallions.

At the time of the Kings, the Salon of Mercury was filled with paintings that are now at the Louvre. Among the most prestigious were *The Entombement* by Titien and *The Holy Family* by Raphael. Of the original furniture, only the curious clock that Antoine Morand presented to the King in 1706 has been returned to its original place. The glazed body reveals the clockwork inside, and automatons move around a bronze statuette representing the King. On its bronze and enamel face, Time has the features of an old man holding a scythe. This room also served as the King's Game Room.

The Salon of Apollo

This room, the last room in the series of State Apartments, was used for two purposes, music and dancing, and on some occasions, audiences granted to ambassadors were held there. The King received them seated on his throne, on a raised platform covered with a Persian rug, facing the windows. The gigantic throne, made of gilded wood, is gone, but one can still see the three eyebolts that held up the canopy above the gold and silver tapestry that has taken its place.

The famous portrait of Louis XIV in his coronation dress painted by Rigaud in 1701 hangs over the mantelpiece. The custom under the monarchy was to place a portrait of the reigning king on the opposite wall. Thus, it is the portrait of the last king at Versailles, Louis XVI in the same dress, painted by Callet, that now faces that of Louis XIV. The walls, which here, too, were adorned with paintings by the Old Masters, such as Rubens or Van Dyck, were covered in winter by crimson velvet with embroidered panels, whereas in summer, the wall hanging was made entirely of gold and silver. It is not hard to imagine the spectacular impression given by a reception in such a room.

Here, as in the two preceding rooms, the bottom of the walls are paneled with dark marble, heightened by white motifs, and the floor is covered with a rug made by the Savonnerie, dating from the 17th century. Six candelabra and a chandelier complete the furnishings. The painted ceiling by Charles de Lafosse crowns the room, presenting a round motif in the center, as in the Salon of Diana. Here, Apollo is depicted on his chariot, accompanied by the Seasons.

Eight gilded stucco sculptures in the round appear to be holding it up. Garlands, swirls and palms form particularly rich compartments, in which four other scenes are painted, with Coriolanus, Vespasian, Augustus and Porus as the heroes. In the corners of the coving, the Four Continents are represented in allegorical form. In these works, the bright colors and graceful shapes already prefigure the development of painting in the 18th century. Lafosse, one of Le Brun's disciples, who was influenced by Rubens, succeeded in softening the noble style of his age.

Preceding pages:
The Hall of Mirrors
Just as Darius wanted the splendor of Persepolis to dazzle his vassals, and the Athenians introduced the Panathenaea Festival when they transferred the treasure of the Delian League to their city, Louis XIV in turn wanted to present an extraordinary display of luxury to his visitors. The Doge of Venice, among many others, brought back memories of the lavish palace of the Sun King before whom he had come to do penance for having lent his support to Spain.

The Salon of War

While the Hall of Mirrors was being built on the former Le Vau terrace, Jules Hardouin-Mansart converted the two rooms that surrounded it. The Salon of Jupiter became the Salon of War in 1678, and its southern counterpart, the Salon of Peace. The three rooms, decorated by Le Brun, bordered the main building of the chateau on the garden side, bringing an extraordinary richness to the State Apartments. The Salon of War, which connected the State Apartments to the Hall of Mirrors, houses as many treasures as the rooms into which it leads.

The walls are covered with green and white marble, adorned with panels of small mirrors, heralding the neighboring Hall of Mirrors. The décor illustrates France's military victories until the Treaty of Nimegen (1678). In the ceiling corners, angels and sunburst emblems look down upon French fleurs-de-lys, surrounded by gilded stucco symbols of war. In the center cupola, Le Brun painted France in arms, surrounded by victories. Seated on a cloud, she carries a shield with an effigy of Louis XIV. In the covings, four half-moon paintings, in dark colors, evoke France's vanquished enemies in allegorical form (Germany, Spain and Holland) as well as Bellona, the Roman goddess of war. Upon entering the room, however, the visitor's eye is immediately drawn to the huge bas-relief in white stucco encircled by pink marble, made by Coysevox.

The sculptor, a favorite of Louis XIV, shows the King on horseback, striking down his enemies. Two allegorical figures of Fame, one offering laurel wreaths and the other blowing a trumpet, stand atop the scene, celebrating his glory, while below, two prisoners weighed down with chains seem to be holding up the entire scene. Beneath it, in a gilded bas-relief, the goddess Clio is writing history. On the terrace surrounding the castle, below the salon, one can see the gigantic War Vase, a work by the same sculptor. Coysevox also produced the funerary monuments of some of the great names at Versailles, such as Colbert and Le Brun, in a style that reveals the influence of both baroque and Greco-Roman art.

The Hall of Mirrors

Though Louis XIV seems to have intended his entire palace as a brilliant symbol of his absolute power, this intention reaches its apotheosis in the Hall of Mirrors. Here, everything was designed to dazzle the visitor's eye and mind: the imposing dimensions, the magnificent materials and works that cover every bit of the walls and ceilings, the long view augmented still further by rigorous symmetry and the play of light reflected in the mirrors.

Mansart was put in charge of erecting the hall in 1678, on the spot where a terrace linking the north and south pavilions of the chateau formerly stood. The following year, Le Brun took over the decorating work, which was to last ten years. The work was not completed until 1689, whereas the Court had already been officially established at Versailles for seven years. The task was monumental: the Hall is 240 feet long, 33 feet wide and 39 feet high. Seventeen immense windows giving onto the gardens bring light into the room, and are reflected in seventeen windows standing opposite, adorned with beveled mirrors in frames of gilded, chiseled copper. The mirror panels comprising them are the largest ones ever produced at the time. The arches are decorated with alternating sunburst emblems and lion skins. Between the windows, pilasters made of red-brown Rance marble are ornamented with gilt bronze bases. The capitals were designed by Caffieri, who invented a "French order" to compete with the classical Ionic and Corinthian orders: the sun is surmounted by a fleur-de-lys, and surrounded by two Gallic roosters against a background of palms. Twenty-four gilded candelabra and forty-one Bohemian crystal chandeliers add to the shimmering of the mirrors.

The barrel vault of the ceiling by Le Brun is the largest single painted expanse in France. The painter was a self-appointed herald of the King's government, from his accession to the throne in 1661 to the Treaty of Nimegen in 1678. "The King gives his orders, the King arms his men on land and sea...", is written across the entire vault, and illustrated by allegories from antiquity. In the center, Louis XIV governing by himself, depicts the King as a young man, surrounded by Graces and children.

In such a grandiose setting, Louis XIV was struck by the almost inordinately sublime idea of creating solid silver furniture. To the great astonishment (and perhaps annoyance) of the Court and the rest of Europe, he was able to obtain it, but only for a short time.

In December 1689, with the War of the League of Augsburg raging, the stools, consoles and every other piece of silver furniture in the State Apartments was sent to the foundry to be melted down: Dangeau noted scrupulously "Not a single piece is left in any of the Apartments." The Hall of Mirrors was then furnished with gilded wood, which was sculpted and carved with such delicacy that, at least from an aesthetic point of view, the furniture was as exquisite as before. Among the porphyry and alabaster vases and busts of Roman emperors, the King displayed the most beautiful pieces in his collection of antiques in the Hall. The Venus of Arles and Diana were placed there in niches surmounted by trophies.

The Hall, which served as a passageway from the King's Apartments to the Queen's, was constantly filled with a highly varied crowd of people. Anyone could circulate freely in the State Apartments, provided they were neither monks nor beggars. Aside from feast days, when coaches coming from Paris created traffic jams on the roads, legions of onlookers came for a glimpse of the royal family and the palace that generated so many rumors. In the hustle and bustle of the corridors, pickpockets went about their work undisturbed, removing snuffboxes and small, precious objects from the members of the Court. The Hall of Mirrors was the setting for many balls, concerts and prestigious suppers. For extraordinary receptions, the throne was set up against the far wall flanked by the Salon of Peace, and visitors were introduced from the other side, which forced them to walk the full eighty yards to reach the King, bowing and curtseying all the while. The throne was placed on a Persian rug with a golden background, encircled by candelabra and silver dishes, and the King was surrounded in great pomp by his children and the high officials of the Court.

In 1871, the King of Prussia received the crown and title of Emperor of Germany in this Hall. Then, in June 1919, Treaty of Versailles was signed here, putting an end to World War I.

The Salon of Peace

With mirrors, green and white marble, a ceiling painted by Le Brun and statues in the Greco-Roman-style, the room echoes the décor of the Salon of War, but with a different set of symbols. Here war trophies give way to round-cheeked cupids and musical instruments. The room, which gives onto the South Parterre, is bathed in light. The cornice with olive branches, ears of wheat and festoons of flowers is adorned with caducei and cornucopias in the angles, surrounded by lyres and surmounted by the crown of France. The gentle atmosphere of peaceful life permeates the entire room .

When the reign of Louis XIV ended, this room was joined to the Queen's Apartments. It was separated from the Hall of Mirrors by a movable wall that was taken out for large receptions. Marie Leszczynska held concerts in this room on a regular basis, where guests heard the music of modern composers such as Rameau, as well as those of the previous century, including Lully and Delalande.

Some evenings were devoted to the "Queen's Games." Like most of her contemporaries, Marie was an ardent gambler, losing huge amounts of money at a game called *cavagnole*. Voltaire witnessed a feverish card game at the royal table in which his friend, Madame du Châtelet took part. He got caught up in the excitement and let slip: "Madame, you are playing with rogues," a remark which earned him a stint in exile.

The ceiling by Le Brun, unlike its counterpart in the Salon of War, features covings in which cherubs reign over Spain, Holland, Germany and Christian Europe. In the center is France, crossing through the air, preceded by Peace, crowned by Glory and accompanied by Hymen.

Above the mantelpiece, as in the other room, hangs a large oval work by Lemoyne, who was to decorate the Salon of Hercules in the same bright colors three years later. This painting of Louis XV giving peace to Europe dates from 1729. At that time, Louis, who was nineteen years old, was still "The Beloved," and the Queen, after bringing three daughters into the world, had just given birth to a dauphin.

The Salon of Peace

This room stands in dazzling symmetry to the Salon of War at the other end of the Hall of Mirrors. It is decorated in marble and dedicated to the political and military successes of the King, who had just concluded the Treaty of Nimegen with Holland.

The Queen's Apartments

Flanked by the Salon of Peace and the Coronation Room, the Queen's Apartments include nine long rooms luxuriously decorated by Le Brun for Queen Marie-Thérèse with the sumptuous marble Queen's Staircase leading up to them.

The Queen's Staircase

The beauty of the multicolored marble that covers the steps, railing and walls and the raised gilded bas-reliefs gives an idea of what the luxurious Ambassador's Staircase, its counterpart in the King's Apartments, must have looked like. The Queen's stairs were built from 1679 to 1681 to match those of her husband. In the large trompe-l'œil perspective work at the top, the figures were painted by Meusnier and the bouquets by Belin de Fontenay.

This staircase led directly to the Queen's Apartments through the Guard Room and that of the King through the Loggia. The courtiers and the curious alike crowded together here during the daytime. Félibien claimed that he knew of "none other as frequented or as well-known at Versailles." Indeed, a constant tumult reigned in the corridors, staircases and hallways of the dream castle. Those with titles could circulate in sedan chairs. Porters had to thread their way between the voluminous panniers of dresses and delicate pumps to deliver their clients to their destinations, which were strictly regulated by Court etiquette. Thus, the daughters of Louis XV had the sole privilege of remaining in their sedans until the Salon of the Oeil-de-Bœuf, whereas everyone else had to leave their sedans in the Guard Room, including the governess who accompanied the princesses. The chronicles of the period report a multitude of examples in which people who had wangled their way through were curtly forced to comply with the rules. In addition, the chateau halls were lined with small shops, carryovers from the former "palace merchants" or "merchants who follow the King" where footmen, courtiers and onlookers could buy lace, flowers and lottery tickets.

The Guardroom

On Holy Thursday, the Queen had thirteen little girls from poor families brought to her room for the washing-of-the-feet ceremony, just as her husband did on his side for boys. After a sermon, the girls were served a meal and each one was given a purse with thirteen ecus. Marie Leszczynska liked to be assisted by her daughters in these rituals dating back to ancient times.

This room was the upper part of the chapel until 1676, when Louis XIV decided to have it enlarged and transferred to what is now the Coronation Room. Le Brun covered the walls of the new Guardroom with predominantly pink-colored marble panels decorated in geometrical patterns, in keeping with the fashion of the 1780s. Noël Coypel (father of Antoine, who painted the dome of the permanent chapel in 1710) was put in charge of painting the ceiling. This elegant room, with overdoors ornamented by graceful white and gold bas-reliefs, in which the door leaves and cornices were decorated with gilded stucco, was filled with solders and arms. The marble floor, which was too fragile for boots and halberds and was constantly being trampled by armies of visitors, was finally replaced by a wooden floor.

The ceiling by Coypel is composed, like all the others, of elaborate, gilded compartments, presenting *Jupiter riding through the air on his chariot*. In an octagonal painting, the god is shown, under the benevolent eye of Piety, surrounded by spirits fighting against the forces of evil. The covings take up the theme of the virtues in four Greco-Roman-style paintings. In the corners, there are unusual trompe-l'oeil paintings in which the courtiers are leaning over a balustrade towards the public below. Two other paintings by Noël Coypel depicting Jupiter adorn the walls. Louis XV sometimes held the "Bed of Justice" in this room. Stands were set up for the public and a platform was reserved for the King.

The Guardroom, which was easily accessible because it was close to the Queen's Staircase, was therefore a strategic point for anyone who wished to be admitted to this part of the palace. It was through this room that the armed, raging Parisians tried to enter the Queen's Bedchamber on October 6, 1789.

The Marble Staircase

This staircase owes its luxury to the Ambassadors' Staircase, for when the latter was completed it appeared quite sober next to its shining new counterpart. It gives an idea of that sumptuous staircase which has since been destroyed.

The Public Dining Room

The red wall hangings and large, brightly colored portraits of the 18th century give warmth to this room, which is lit up by four chandeliers. The room, which was originally the Queen's Guardroom, has retained traces of its past, such as the decoration of the trophy cornice. Vignon's painting of *Mars seated on his Chariot* was removed from the ceiling in the 19th century, but the covings are still adorned with monochromes of warriors. This was the stronghold of the Queen's footmen, where courtiers waited to be admitted to an audience.

The Queen dined here with her husband, in the presence of the courtiers and the public, who stood behind a balustrade. Marie-Thérèse and Marie Leszczynska came here every day; Marie-Antoinette followed the custom as long as she was the Dauphine but relaxed the rules thereafter. She would gladly have had the marble replaced by wood paneling, as in the Salon of the Nobles, but her many remodeling projects were only partially completed. Hence, this room has not changed since the time of Marie-Thérèse. When Marie-Antoinette gave balls here, the Mars painting was hidden behind a false ceiling, and the musicians were put in stands set up against one of the walls. Beginning in 1671, plays were presented here on a small, portable stage.

It was on the occasion of a Public Dinner that young Mozart played for Louis XV on January 1, 1764. The seven-year-old child, accompanied by his father and his sister, won the heart of Marie Leszczynska, who acted as his interpreter with the King. Wolfgang also impressed the French princesses, for whom he composed a few sonatas. A huge painting by the famous portraitist, Madame Vigée-Lebrun, hanging opposite the fireplace, immediately draws the visitor's attention. This is the most famous portrait of Marie-Antoinette, surrounded by her children (Madame Royale, the Duc de Normandie and the Dauphin). It was painted two years before the Revolution in the Salon of Peace.

Madame Adélaïde, the third daughter of Louis XV (one of the three sisters raised at Versailles), and Madame Victoire, surround their mother in another portrait.

The Salon of the Nobles

This room looks more or less as it did in the time of Marie-Antoinette. The ceiling, painted by Michel Corneille in 1671, is the sole vestige of the original décor, produced for Marie-Thérèse. Everything else was remodeled by the Queen's favorite architect, Mique, at the birth of the future Louis XVII, in 1785. Marie-Antoinette wanted to modernize the décor of this antechamber, while limiting the expense. She chose pale green silk with a floral pattern to cover the walls and wood paneling on the lower part, painted white with gold fillets. Twelve matching stools stand in a row around the room.

The blue Turquin marble mantelpiece, with bronzes by Gouthière, holds up one of the three large mirrors adorning the room. The two corner cupboards and two commodes by Reisener, which were made for the room, are now back in their original places. Even the andirons have been faithfully reproduced, and the chandelier, like the Savonnerie rug, is a period piece. A tapestry by Cozette – a rarity at Versailles – based on the famous portrait of Louis XV by Van Loo, hangs among the paintings by Boucher.

Formal presentations to the Queen took place in this room, according to a ritual that continued all the way to the Tuileries, after the night of October 5, 1789. The lady to be presented, accompanied by her parents or lady friends, had to bow before the Queen in keeping with a pre-determined number of curtsies. The Queen also held the meetings of her "circle" in this room. Louis XIV would have liked his wife to be as skillful as Anne of Austria had been at this exercise, which he considered one of the important tasks required of her royal position.

The "salons" held at the hotels of Rambouillet, Albret and Richelieu were concentrated at Versailles during her reign. These salons were not just sophisticated events where wit rivaled with beauty; they were also an occasion to see and be seen and to keep up to date on the news as well as the latest episodes in the destinies of everyone at the Court. After the death of Marie-Thérèse, the Duchesse de Bourgogne kept these rooms alive for a time, and then they remained deserted until the arrival of Marie Leszczynska.

The Queen's Bedchamber

Queen Marie-Thérèse lived in this room, which was decorated for her by Le Brun, for only one year. Louis XIV then gave it to his grandson's wife, the Duchesse de Bourgogne, who gave birth to the future Louis XV here in 1719. The latter, like the other eighteen royal children who came into the world at Versailles, was born in public, according to an ancient tradition.

When Marie Leszczynska arrived in 1725, Versailles had not had a queen for forty years, yet she received a cold welcome. "The hearts of the French are not made to love Poles, who are Northern Gascons and very republican," said Marais. The marriage may have caused a sensation, but in actual fact, it was the status of Marie's father, more than her nationality, that unsettled the minds of the bourgeoisie and the Court in the 18th century.

According to Barbier, Stanislas Leszczynski, placed on the throne of Poland by the Swedish in 1704, and forced into exile when the country was defeated by the Russians in 1709, was not even from "one of the four great houses of the Polish nobility." The disappointment was all the greater as the first woman intended for Louis XV, the daughter of the King of Spain who was already living at Versailles, possessed all the desirable noble characteristics. Her only fault was her young age, in view of the fact that the Prime Minister, the Duc de Bourbon, decided in 1725 it was urgent that the King have descendents. The wedding was quickly expedited: in early March, a message was sent to Madrid indicating that the Infante was being sent home; on March 31, after examining the various possibilities, all of them ruled out for religious or diplomatic reasons, Stanislas was informed that his daughter had been selected; on August 15, the Duc d'Orleans wed Marie in Reims, in the name of the King; on September 5, Louis XV himself married her in Fontainbleau.

Marie Leszczynska was twenty-two years old, and had been carefully educated. As a result, she was able to adapt with good grace to her unexpected position, despite any reticence that her arrival may have caused. One odd detail, reported by her contemporaries: the King was faithful to her for eight years; and he conveyed his

attachment by the embellishments made in her apartments, especially her Bedchamber. When, after giving birth to three daughters, the Queen finally produced an heir in 1729, Louis XV ordered the room to be redecorated. The new design was made by Robert de Cotte and completed by Gabriel and his son, six years later. The King was eager to make it a splendid room, typical of his time. The paneling by Verberckt, Dugoulon and Le Goupil is filled with stones, palms and flowers mixed in with white and gold.

The ceiling of mythological subjects by Gilles de Sève was softened by a composition by Boucher: four monochromes presenting Charity, Fidelity, Plenty and Prudence surrounded by stones, palms and gilded cupids.

The Jewel Casket
The remarkable jewel casket made by Schwerdfger and offered to the Queen by the City of Paris in 1787 now stands next to the bed. The caryatides and Greek motifs of the miniatures already suggest the Empire style to come, whereas the straight legs, ornamented with gilt bronze garlands are unmistakably in the style of Louis XIV. The many mother-of-pearl and porcelain inlays combined with the gilding match the tones of the bedchamber.

The overdoors by Natoire and Jean-François de Troy are also richly and gracefully sculpted. Louis XV, in his role as an attentive young husband, granted the Queen a high household standard, investing enormous amounts of money in replacing her linens every three years. Marie Leszczynska enjoyed various decors during the forty-three years she spent here. These commissions constituted a substantial subsidy for the manufactures of Lyon as well as a tribute to her husband, the King. In 1668, when she died in her bed, she had produced two heirs and eight daughters. Two years later, a fifteen-year-old Dauphine came to take her place.

Marie-Antoinette had just married the future Louis XVI, before becoming Queen of France in 1774, at the death of Louis XV. There was no longer any question of sobriety: Marie-Antoinette had no intention of contenting herself with a walk-on role. At first, the changes she introduced were modest: she added the two-headed eagle of the House of Austria to the coats-of-arms of France and Navarre in the ceiling corners; then she replaced the portraits of the Marie Leszczynska's family with those of her own family members.

After a few necessary repairs (changing the hardwood floor, touching up the gilding), Marie-Antoinette finally decided she wanted to redecorate it completely. She had crimson and gold wall hangings made for winter, with the gathering and embroidery she favored and adorned the windows with pelmets and tieback curtains. For summer, she ordered blue and white brocade with flowers and butterflies, but when it was put up, it no longer satisfied her. She then chose white Tours brocade embroidered with bouquets of flowers, with intertwining ribbons and peacock feathers.

The room belonged to Marie-Antoinette for nineteen years, until she was forced to leave it at dawn on October 6, 1789, under the pressure of rioters. The fences and gates of Versailles, which were normally open, and the guards who were more accustomed to serving than to fighting, were unable to hold back the crowd that had come from Paris and camped overnight in the courtyards. The Queen was able to flee by the small door still visible next to the Jewel Casket, to join her husband.

The Queen's Private Cabinets

The King possessed large private apartments, whereas the rooms to which the Queen could retire were small and gave onto an inner courtyard. The decor we see today is a reproduction of the setting in which Marie-Antoinette enjoyed her hours of freedom. She received her close friends and suppliers, seamstresses and hairdressers, without any of the compulsory reserve imposed in the Queen's Apartments. She sat for Madame Vigée-Lebrun, her official portrait painter, in the Gilded Cabinet, with its paneling by the Rousseau brothers.

She also had a library built, but the most famous of all the Cabinet rooms is the Meridian Cabinet, where the Queen rested in the afternoon. This room was redecorated for Marie-Antoinette by Mique, her First Architect. His décor of white, gold and pale blue made the small, octagonal room a haven of freshness, just a few steps away from the official Bedchamber.

The Meridian Cabinet
This delightful small drawing room suggests the happier times of Marie-Antoinette, when she had just offered France her first son, the Dauphin.

The paneling and furniture, with their flower garlands, hearts and dolphins mixed together with fleurs-de-lys are a reminder of the fact that the renovation took place in 1781, on the occasion of the birth of the first Dauphin.

The Apartments of Madame de Maintenon

The four rooms occupied by Madame de Maintenon on the first floor testify to her special status at the Court. The apartments, which were connected to the King's Apartments by the Loggia, and were in the vicinity of the Queen's Apartments, reveal her position as the morganatic Queen, recognized, if not officially at least unquestionably, as the King's wife.

The destiny of Françoise d'Aubigné, the granddaughter of the poet Agrippa d'Aubigné, was like a novel in more ways than one. There was nothing in her childhood as a poor orphan or her adoption by a family of Calvinists to prepare Madame de Maintenon to become the companion of King Louis XIV in his later years or the symbol of Catholic France in Versailles. The death of her husband, the writer Scarron, forced her to find various forms of employment, until she was entrusted with the education of the children of Madame de Montespan and the King.

The Marquise de Montespan, compromised in a case of poisoning, was then slowly ousted, and Louis XIV married Madame de Maintenon in secret, shortly after the Queen's death in 1683. The secret was so well kept that historians wonder where the marriage took place, some situating it in one of the cabinets, others in the Chapel. The reality of the marriage, however, seems beyond doubt. For thirty-two years, Louis XIV was to come every day to visit her in these apartments giving onto the Royal Courtyard. Sitting down in an armchair, the King often worked with a minister or an advisor, while Madame de Maintenon stayed in the background, doing needlepoint or reading. According to witnesses, the sovereign sometimes asked her questions, listening carefully to the opinions she expressed with great restraint. Saint-Simon himself acknowledged her discretion, despite the fierce portrait he drew of her: "She thought and felt so very small in all things, that she was always less than Madame Scarron." Mademoiselle de Scudéry, on the contrary, found that she had "sparkling dark eyes, full of passion and wit."

Although Madame de Maintenon's influence has often been judged harshly, and she has been held responsible for the austere atmosphere of the latter part of the reign of Louis XIV, as well as for decisions such as the revocation of the Edict of Nantes, she was the driving force behind a number of generous enterprises. With the support of the pastor of Notre Dame Church and a few good souls, such as Madame de Rochefoucauld (one of her faithful allies), she set up the "City Charity", to help the disadvantaged. She organized relief for those suffering from cold and hunger during the terrible winter of 1709. To finance her charitable undertakings, she sold some of her personal possessions.

Finally, Madame de Maintenon was, above all, the "Lady of Saint-Cyr." In 1686, she founded a school on the edge of the palace gardens for the young daughters of noble families who had lost their fortunes. The institution took up much of her time during the last years of her life. After the King's death, she retired there to devote herself to prayer. Three years older than Louis XIV, she died in 1719 at the age of eighty-four. Her apartments, once emptied in order to be converted into a museum by Louis-Philippe, have since been entirely refurnished with 17th century pieces.

The King's Apartments

To reach the King's Apartments, it was necessary to take the Queen's Staircase leading to the King's Guardroom, followed by the Antechamber of the Public Dining Room. Then, crossing through the Salon of the Oeil-de-Bœuf, the King's Bedchamber and the Council Cabinet, one arrived at the King's Private Apartments. The King himself enjoyed greater freedom of movement, as he could use the Ambassadors' Staircase whenever he wished to go directly to his Apartments.

The Guardroom

The Guardroom was, by definition, intended for the guards of the King's Household. It was decorated with relatively simply wood paneling and functional furniture, including guard benches and beds, and racks for arms. A beautiful cornice adorned with warrior attributes and a painting above the mantelpiece recall the purpose of the room.

On Mondays, a table was set up, covered with a red velvet rug with gold fringe, on which anyone who so desired could place a petition intended for the King. For a while, Louis XIV attended this event in person, and later he put Louvois in charge. The "petition table" then became a mere mailbox.

The Public Dining Room

Here Louis XIV had "supper" (which corresponded to our dinner) in public, alone after the death of the Queen and the Dauphine. He sat with his back to the fireplace, in a "table armchair," facing the gallery of musicians who often accompanied his meals.

When his grandson, the Duc d'Anjou, was promised the Crown of Spain, he was sometimes admitted to the table. At the end of his reign, and during those that followed, the room was given over to footmen, in charge of identifying the people who introduced themselves before entering the Salon of the *Oeil-de-Bœuf* or Bull's Eye Window.

The Salon of the Bull's-Eye Window

This celebrated room occupied a strategic point in the King's palace: it was the last station before the Royal Bedchamber. The antechamber, which was decorated by Mansart and Robert de Cotte (at the same time as work on the Chapel began), is significant of a new trend.

Forty years after the first construction work at Versailles, the King's tastes had evolved, and probably those of the artists as well. While there was some concern about saving money, since France's fortunes were no longer on the rise as they had been in the 1670s, economics was only one factor. The style of Louis XV is perceptible in the swirls and curves, when the refinement of the work was as important as the prestige of the materials used. The Salon of the Bull's-Eye Window, the Bedchamber and the Council Cabinet all have plain white ceilings, decorated with gilded moldings. Here there was no marble on the walls, but white wood paneling instead, which was sumptuously elaborate and gilded, and in the other two rooms, magnificent fabrics to give them a warmer look.

When Louis XV had his Bedchamber set up where we see it today, the former bedchamber was joined to the Salon of the Bassans to produce this antechamber of the Bull's-Eye, which received its name from the oval dormer window ornamenting the attic. The influence of Versailles on people's minds was so great that Royal antechambers were often given such names for no good reason. Beautiful mirrors reflect the three chandeliers that lit up the crowd of visitors pressing against each other to be the first to enter for the King's Rising and Retiring ceremonies. Here, too, visitors lay in wait for him when he went to see his wife. When the King left his Bedchamber, announced by the usher, it was important to be standing as close as possible in order to make requests or utter compliments, or merely to be observed and therefore remembered by the sovereign. During these long waiting periods, the courtiers spent their time in conversations during which the reputations of the Court were often made or ruined. When Louis XIV was ill at the end of his life, he had music played in this room in the evening, whereas under Louis XV, sparkling feasts were held here to celebrate the engagement of the daughter of the King of Spain to the Duc de Chartres.

**Louis XIV
as a Greek god**

The painting by Jean Nocret depicts the royal family as divinities on Mount Olympus. On the right, Marie-Thérèse is represented more in keeping with the portrait seen at the rear of the room. The famous dormer window in the attic of the ceiling, which is shaped like a bull's-eye, gives its name to this antechamber where courtiers awaited the Rising of the King.

The King's Bedchamber

In 1701, Louis XIV had his Bedchamber set up in the center of his Household. Under Louis XII, this room had been the State Room of the chateau, with three windows giving onto the Marble Courtyard and three large windows overlooking the terrace. When the terrace was converted into the Hall of Mirrors in 1678, the windows had to be closed and the decoration entirely renovated. For many years, it was the "Room where the King gets dressed", with the King's Bedchamber situated at the corner of the Marble Courtyard. Later in life, Louis XIV had it turned into a ceremonial chamber, and this magnificent complex was designed for him, in which even the most humble keyhole is hidden by the artistry of bronze sculptors.

The white walls and fabrics gleam with gold; there are friezes everywhere, with floral motifs, cupids and delicately fluted pilasters. The overdoors are adorned with medallions (by Van Eyck, among others), framed by round-bosse sculptures of gilded stucco. The mirror frame is also covered with copiously carved gold leaf and for the first time, the top of a mirror was rounded. Around the room, four paintings are built into the attic, which makes the room exceptionally tall. (There were nine works by Valentin de Boulogne, in the vein of Caravaggio before the remodeling in 1701). Finally, behind a balustrade of gilded wood, the King's bed occupies the center of one wall, surmounted by a carved, gilded motif by Coustou: *France watching over the Sleeping Monarch*. The carving stands out from a gold background crisscrossed with flowerets, similar to the covings of the Salon of the Bull's-Eye Window.

In 1980, the winter furnishings of crimson velvet heavily laden with gold and stylized motifs were reconstructed. The original ones were used for more than eighty years, until the time of Louis XVI, and when the fabric grew too dilapidated and was finally burned, it yielded one hundred and thirty-two pounds of the precious metal. To reconstruct the bed curtains, the counterpanes, the hangings for the canopy and the rear of the alcove and chair seat coverings, the Lyon manufacture recovered its former aura for a time. Looms that had long sat idle were put back into use and the weavers employed ancient techniques to make the brocades of genuine gold and silver more authentic. Lyon had the privilege of making "gold and silk sheets" since Louis XI. In the 16th century, François I granted the manufacture a monopoly on importing and selling silk. Fabric has rarely been treated to such an extent as a noble material, on a par with marble and crystal. Armchairs and stools were covered in silk re-embroidered with gold, reflecting the desire for splendor in even the most ordinary objects. In the summer, the walls and the entire canopy bed were adorned with light green brocade with flowers and silver thread. The sumptuously decorated bed, located at the heart of the castle, was so charged with symbolic meaning that, during the reign of Louis XIV, anyone who crossed the room during the day saluted it.

The courtiers' day began and ended here, regulated at all times by the monarch. The first valet was given the responsibility of waking the King. Then, his doctor entered, accompanied by members of the royal family and senior palace officials. At 8:15 a.m., the first gentleman of the Bedchamber opened the bed curtain, and the courtiers were then admitted. After being shaved by the royal barber, the King dressed, with the help of a few privileged courtiers, and then said his prayers, assisted by the grand chaplain. Then he gave private audiences received the representatives of the provinces, who came to present him with their requests and grievances. At night, the same ritual took place when it was time to retire. When the King undressed, the courtiers withdrew, leaving the sovereign with the colonel of his guards. The King then got into bed, in the presence of members of the royal family and senior palace officials who in turn withdrew, leaving only a prince or two to share the relative privacy, taking advantage of the opportunity to discuss personal business. At bedtime, each courtier was eager to be granted the special honor of holding the candle to light the King. Even Saint-Simon, who was always quick to mock, was not averse to this task as "the King had such an art of making something out of nothing."

The Bedchamber was also used as a Small Dining Room. After the Council, at about 1 p.m., the sovereign would sit down at a small, square table covered with a damask tablecloth, facing the middle window. In keeping with a tradition dating back to Charlemagne, the King ate alone at his table, but he sometimes invited his brother to join him. The meal, like all the occupations of Louis XIV at Versailles, was a spectacle. Curious courtiers edged their way through the open doors to within a few yards of the King, occupying the entire antechamber and the adjoining rooms. Lunch was another occasion for the sovereign to chat with selected interlocutors: every remark he made and every reply he received was then the subject of commentary among the courtiers. Whenever he had a pleasant word for someone, asked a question or ostensibly ignored someone he usually talked to, his attitude was analyzed and his remarks were interpreted, in an effort to detect the honor or disgrace that was in the making.

The ordinary menu was composed of three courses: soup, main dishes such as leg of lamb, cooked ham, capon, etc. and entremets including omelets, vegetables, pâté, fruit, etc. The King's meals occupied more than three hundred people, working in the Grand Commons, both in the kitchen and performing related tasks such as overseeing the ovens, the candelabra, bread, tableware and linens, cup bearers and wine waiters, and a myriad of kitchen boys, all under the surveillance of the General Controller of Food, who managed the provisions. Between dishes, the King was handed a damp napkin. The fork had not yet come into widespread use, so the King had only a knife and a spoon. The rules present throughout the Court were repeated here in their minutest details. The carved silver serving dishes were always placed on the royal table in perfect symmetry, with an implacable sense of decorum. Each one was the occasion for a veritable procession of a dozen people, lined up in a strict order, from the Grand Master of the King's Household to the keeper of the dish, all of them gentlemen for whom this responsibility was a distinction. In the midst of such profuse refinement, reasons of state nevertheless had their place: the King did not eat or drink until after his tasters, and when a glass was brought to him, it was always covered. At the end of the royal meal, the courtiers hurried back to their own apartments to eat in turn, before changing their clothes to attend the hunt.

On September 1, 1715, Louis XIV died in this room, where he had lived for fourteen years, after a reign of seventy-two years. Under Louis XV, the room would serve only an official purpose. At the end of the life of the Sun King, the State Apartments had taken on

an almost sacred character, and the setting that Louis XIV had created for himself was too closely assimilated with the Great King himself for anyone to think of modifying it. Yet times had changed and the 18th century was more sensitive to the new notion of comfort. The Bedchamber, due to its size and aspect, could never be anything but poorly heated, and on some winter days, the water froze on the King's table. Louis XV (like Louis XVI after him) continued to come here for ceremonies but no longer slept in this room. He had his private bedchamber set up in the former Billiard Room of his great-grandfather, which faced south and was a more convenient size. He nevertheless had a fireplace added to the Ceremonial Chamber, which had only one under Louis XIV. While strictly observing the same etiquette, he introduced a certain amount of flexibility in the timetable. Sometimes his chaplain would be found sitting down, tired out from waiting so long, something unthinkable under Louis XIV. Louis XVI, in his great renovation project, nearly broke away from tradition by relocating the official chamber, but he had neither the finances nor the time to do so.

Until the Revolution, all the sovereigns perpetuated in the same setting each detail of the Rising and Retiring ritual introduced by the monarch whose stamp upon palace life seemed quite indelible.

Louis XIV by Coysevox

This room was originally planned as a salon and was not intended to be lived in. Louis XIV moved his private quarters here in 1701, in compliance with a very ancient tradition that required the King's bedchamber to be located in the heart of the castle. By 1738, Louis XV kept the room only for the ritual ceremonies of Rising and Retiring. In 1761, he had a second fireplace installed. A bust of Louis XIV, carved by Antoine Coysevox, was placed on one of the mantelpieces.

The Council Chamber

Versailles, known for its feasts and ceremonies, was first and foremost the seat of government for a hundred years. In this cabinet, the monarchs and their ministers determined the history of France, from 1682 to the end of the Old Regime.

The room, which was originally decorated with mirrors, was enlarged under Louis XV by Jacques-Ange Gabriel to include a small adjoining room: the Wig Room, also known as the Statue Room. The architect himself designed the motif of the paneling, which was handsomely carved by Antoine Rousseau: each panel evokes a different attribute of the Council, presenting trophies of peace, war, the navy, justice, etc. Huge mirrors light up the white walls and ceiling, heightened by gilding.

The overdoors by Verdier and Houasse, a bust of Alexander covered with gilt bronze by Garardon, and a Scipion carved by Coustou add to the pure rococo décor. The tablecloth and blue satin curtains with gold brocade were woven according to a pattern produced for Louis XV, who also had a fireplace of griotte marble embellished with bronze installed in the room.

Under Louis XIV, the furniture included a daybed which, according to Dangeau, allowed him "to stay here during the daytime, if his illness [his tumor] forced him to lie down; this room was the farthest removed from noise." Every morning, the king came here to give "the orders to each one for the day", and then, when he came back from Mass, he would listen to the reports of his ministers.

In his *Memoirs* written for his son, Louis XIV noted: "nothing is more dangerous than a king who is usually sleeping, and wakes from time to time, after losing track of affairs, and who then blames on everyone else the ill fortune for which he should accuse himself."

The Council of State or the High Council was held three or four times a week. Only the State ministers attended with the King, to discuss the important issues of domestic and foreign policy. In 1661, when Fouquet was

disgraced, his title of Superintendent of Finances disappeared along with him. Louis XIV replaced it by a Finance Council, which met twice a week, under the aegis of one of the leading Council heads, such as Colbert, Le Tellier or his son, Louvois.

At the Correspondence Council, held once a fortnight, the King sometimes invited the Dauphin, his brother or a few privileged individuals. In his fifty-four years of personal reign, Louis XIV proved exceptionally faithful, as he had only sixteen State Ministers, six Chancellors, Six General Comptrollers of Finance, five State Secretaries of War, five of Foreign Affairs and four

The Council Chamber

The room now looks much the way it did when Louis XV and Louis XVI met here with their ministers. The beautiful blue and gold satin covering the table, the curtains and the stools was woven according to a pattern selected by Louis XV.

of the Navy. Some of these men held several positions simultaneously. Thursdays were ordinarily set aside for audiences with the Building staff, household valets and gardeners, whereas the King devoted Friday mornings to his confessor. Finally, the Private Council, with the Chancellor presiding, was held once a month, bringing together thirty State Councilors and ninety-eight rapporteurs or Masters of the Petitions to prepare Edicts and Government Orders.

The Council Chamber was also the setting for official audiences and the place where the sovereign received ladies for their first appearance at the Court, as well as courtiers to whom he extended congratulations or condolences, depending on the circumstances. From time to time, music was played for the King's enjoyment (Louis XIV had a harpsichord installed), or a writer was brought in to read extracts from his works. The courtiers, amassed in the adjoining room, took advantage of the entertainment.

Here, the Duc d'Anjou, the great-grandson of Louis XIV, was pronounced King of Spain in 1700. Louis XVI received Monsieur de Brézé, who came to tell him that the deputies were resisting his orders, as well as Mirabeau's famous reply on June 23, 1789.

The King's private Apartments

Like all the official rooms, the King's private apartments were significantly transformed, in accordance with the tastes and needs of each sovereign. In spite of the importance Louis XIV attached to his public life, he had private apartments set up for himself as soon as the State Apartments were finished. The section situated between the Council Chamber and the Salon of Abundance was set aside for salons devoted to relaxation (Billiard Room, the Library and the Oval Salon). The few intimates who were allowed access to these rooms were the subject of lively jealousy among the courtiers. Saint-Simon grudgingly mentions "the audiences unknown from the behinds."

The private apartments nevertheless kept the imprint of the personality of the King, an avid collector of precious objects. Books, paintings, gems and carved bronzes were in view everywhere, turning the apartments into a genuine museum in which each room was decorated to enhance the royal collections. The King liked to visit with foreign guests and knowledgeable amateurs, artists and scientists who were capable of appreciating the rare objects on display.

Before Louis XV satisfied his aesthetic taste, he began by ensuring a degree of comfort in this private space that was lacking in the rest of the palace. He also enjoyed finding respite here from the constraints of public life. He created his private bedchamber in 1738 and somewhat modified the order of the rooms. Finally, Louis XVI introduced new décors and increased the private character of this area by having a Back Cabinet installed.

The Bedchamber of Louis XV

Louis XV had been reigning at Versailles for sixteen years when he felt the need for a private bedchamber. Only the Council Cabinet separated it from the Ceremonial Chamber that his great-grandfather had occupied. When Louis XV had the Billiard Room of Louis XIV (also called the Antechamber of the Dogs) enlarged, he had a private bedchamber created as well. The Rising and Retiring ceremonies continued to take place in the Ceremonial Chamber, whereas the private bedchamber was for sleeping.

In this more human-sized setting, which he had completely renovated according to his tastes, he could hope to enjoy some form of rest. Privacy was only relative at Versailles, for a valet slept on a folding bed beside the King. In keeping with ancient custom, all activity ceased while the King slept. Coaches were prevented from entering courtyards, emptied of their occupants. Time was suspended until the monarch rose.

Louis XV decorated his new bedchamber sumptuously. The wood paneling was designed by Gabriel and carved by Verberckt. The alcove and the entire room were adorned with fabrics woven in Lyon by the finest craftsmen. An inventory of the bedchamber furnishings suggests a constant battle against the cold, including bed curtains, a screen, portieres and double curtains at the windows.

The two magnificent clocks surrounding the alcove disappeared, like many other pieces, during the Revolution. Among them was a chest of drawers with carved bronzes by Caffieri and a few masterpieces by 18th-century goldsmiths, such as the large candelabra by Germain and two sugar bowls by Roettiers, weighing almost seven pounds each.

Louis XV died in this room on May 10, 1774. He suddenly felt ill at the Trianon, and was brought to the palace for the final moments of his life. He was the only King of France who was born in Versailles and died there, after living a total of fifty-seven years, interrupted only by the seven years of the Regency. Although the King had been affectionately nicknamed "The Beloved", the end of his reign was surrounded by controversy and he had to be duried at night in secret, for fear of rioting.

The Clock Cabinet

When Louis XV inaugurated his bedchamber, he had a gaming room set up in the adjoining space, which is known today as the Clock Cabinet. Originally, this

cabinet had a semi-circular wall inlaid with astronomical clocks, which immediately gave their name to the room. Twenty-two years later, the other clocks were removed and the wood paneling was entirely remodeled in order to install the masterpiece by Passemant. The refined décor of the mirrors and carved paneling that one sees today show no signs of the conversion work, due to the talent of Verberckt.

The Passemant clock is worthy of a room of its own. The Duc de Luynes considered it "the most beautiful shape in the world (…) with a globe above, in which one sees the sun represented as a golden sphere in the center and all the planets revolving around with such precision that the clockmaker says it cannot go out of order for ten thousand years."

The King had this wonderful piece set up in Versailles in 1754, before sealing it with a marble base on which it stands today. The case made of gilt bronze and designed by Caffieri holds a clock that the famous clockmaker, Dauthiau, spent a dozen years producing under the direction of Passemant. The result was altogether revolutionary: "it can run for six weeks," noted Luynes. More amazing still, the clock also showed the day, the month and the year as well as the phases of the moon. Louis XV loved to watch the prodigious spectacle that took place every December 31 when the New Year was displayed.

The end of the 18th century was marked by important scientific and technological progress, which were of great interest to the King, and to his grandson after him. While Newton's theories were being refined, Réamur continued his work, Roubo published his *Dictionary of Carpentry*, Diderot and d'Alemebert gathered together a group of philosophers, scientists and specialists in various fields to produce the *Encylopédie*, the *Dictionnaire raisonné des sciences, des arts et des métiers*.

Passemant's clock

This masterpiece of clockwork showed not only the time but also the position of the planets in a globe surmounted by the clock face. The clock, acknowledged to be Passemant's masterpiece, was in fact the result of teamwork.

The Corner Room

Under Louis XIV, this room was used as a billiard room and then as his Picture Room where the King displayed his collection of crystal in addition to his favorite paintings. At the time, the room had two large windows and the walls were covered with red damask and gold trim. Louis XV began renovating this room in 1738 by having the windows closed up. The following year, he had a Medal Cabinet installed, sumptuously adorned with gilt bronzes, which he had commissioned from Gaudreaux. One window of the room gives out onto the Royal Courtyard and another gives onto the Marble Courtyard. From this view looking down onto the surroundings, it was easy to control the comings and goings of visitors. That was undoubtedly one of the reasons it was so much appreciated by the King, who spent more and more time here working.

In 1753, he decided to turn it into a real work cabinet, putting Gabriel in charge of the new decor. The walls were covered with paneling carved by Verberckt: the ten large panels sculpted with children's games are among his most beautiful creations. First, Louis XV had a red lacquered desk made, and then in 1760, he ordered a cylinder-top desk, which is now the centerpiece of the room. Two of the greatest 18th century cabinetmakers worked together on this piece: Oeben and Riesener. Oeben, who had been the King's cabinetmaker since 1754, died before completing the work; Riesener, who was his pupil before he married Oeben's widow and took over the workshop, finished the task in 1769. Oeben, who enjoyed the protection of Madame de Pompadour and Riesener, who often worked for Marie-Antoinette, created many other pieces of furniture with mechanisms, which were highly prized at the time, but this one is unquestionably a masterpiece of elegance and technique.

Once the cylinder was locked, the "desk of secrets" (the word "secretary" appeared in 1765) was a safe place for Louis XV, where he kept his red book with a list of the members of the King's Secret. Every day the King held interviews here, which were less solemn than in the Council Chamber. It was also in this room that the Post Office Superintendent came to deliver the information gleaned from letters read in the Cabinet Noir. Louis XVI also spent long hours in this room.

The desk of Louis XV

This famous cylinder-top desk, begun by Oeben and completed by Riesener, is considered one of the masterpieces of the art of marquetry. It is one of the few pieces of furniture at Versailles, which did not suffer during the shifting events of the Revolution, and hence was able to remain in its original setting.

The New Rooms

These rooms were given the name "New Rooms" during the reign of Louis XV. Previously, the apartment of Madame de Montespan was located here, until Louis XIV decided to move her to the ground floor. The King then took advantage of the space to convert the domain of his former favorite into a display room for his pictures and precious gems.

In 1684, a suite of small salons called the Small Gallery had their ceilings painted by Mignard. The walls were covered with damask, and hung with celebrated paintings, which were often changed according to the wishes of the sovereign. Among them was, for a time, the *Mona Lisa*. This room, which Louis XIV liked to have his visitors admire, was sometimes called the Gem Room. A description dating from 1687 gives an idea of the luxury: "There is a prodigious quantity of beautiful agates adorned with diamonds (…) . One sees gifts from the Siamese and from the ambassadors of China."

This small museum disappeared in 1752, along with its precious ceiling, when Louis XV decided to remodel the Gallery into dwelling rooms in order to house Madame Adélaïde.

The only apartment that remains is Madame Adélaïde's Music Room where Mozart performed as a child for the daughters of Louis XV. Then, in 1769, Louis XV integrated these rooms into his Inner Apartments and they were given the name "New Rooms."

At the end of every year, in the Dining Room of the New Rooms, courtiers came to admire and buy the latest creations of the Manufacture de Sèvres. The custom continued under Louis XVI, who often had his "small supper" here, surrounded by his family. He had the red damask wall covering replaced by fabric in which the blue matched that of the porcelain adorning the walls.

The hunting scenes with their fresh tones adopted motifs created by Oudry, which were first used for tapestries. Louis XVI innovated again in 1775 by creating a Gaming Room in what had formerly been the Cabinet of Curiosities of Louis XIV and then the antechamber of Madame Adélaïde.

In the four corners, one can still see pieces of furniture characteristic of the end of the 18th century, that Riesener made for the occasion, along with chairs by Boulard in pure Louis XVI style.

The Dining Room of the New Rooms

Also known as the Porcelain Dining Room, this room was recently restored, giving visitors an idea of private royal living. Louis XV attached great importance to the porcelains cherished by Madame de Pompadour, and encouraged the development of the porcelain trade.

The Library of Louis XVI

This room was first the bedchamber of Madame Adélaïde, the third daughter of Louis XV, before it was transformed into a gaming room. When Louis XVI decided to turn it into a library, it was the first renovation he ordered after taking the throne in 1774. Gabriel, who by then was seventy years old, conducted the remodeling work brilliantly. The woodwork was entrusted to the ornamental sculptor Rousseau, whereas a bookseller, Fournier, decorated the doors with imitation bookbindings.

The fireplaces at Versailles often have a history of their own; this one comes from a salon belonging to Madame du Barry at the Chateau of Fontainbleau. The white marble was carved by Boizot, the great bisque sculptor of Sèvres, and adorned with finely sculpted bronzes. The furniture, including tables, a secretary and a chest of drawers, is signed by Riesener, Roentgen and Bennemann.

Louis XVI had a preference for this room where, witnesses tell us, he had books, blueprints and papers scattered about in disorder. The catalogue of titles in the library has come down to us, along with a number of the books themselves. Louis acquired an *Encylopédie*, with its supplements, in 1777. Science had become the main center of interest since the beginning of the century, exceeding metaphysics. The last King of Versailles, who is sometimes presented as not very clever and inclined to do-it-yourself occupations, was eager to learn about all the scientific and geographical discoveries of his time.

In his "workshop" cabinets, which he called "his towers," Louis XVI spent his time at carpentry and making clocks and locks, as well as at physics and mechanics. The rooms he occupied were filled with strange clocks, thermometers, various instruments and maps of all kinds. Louis XVI, a contemporary of Cook and Bougainville, launched the expedition of La Pérouse himself, in 1785.

The Library of Louis XVI

This room is a fine example of the style of Louis XVI, and corresponds quite well to the personality of its master. The King was keen on faraway expeditions, and had an interesting collection of books, which is known to us through the inventory. The world map which is on display here today was the one he looked at when he was following the sea voyages of his cherished vessel, La Pérouse.

The Coronation Room

Louis-Philippe found in this former Great Room of the Queen's Guards a location worthy of the two paintings by David, *The Crowning of the Emperor and Empress Josephine* and *The Army taking the Oath after the Distribution of Eagles*. The exceptional size of these works forced him to raise the ceiling. *The Coronation*, a model for history paintings, is 20 feet long and 30 feet wide. It therefore had to be hung in the largest room in the palace. The original painting was brought to the Louvre for the World Fair in 1889, but the copy at Versailles was also done by the painter himself, who started it in 1808 and finished it in 1822 during his exile in Brussels. Pope Pius VII, who had come from Rome for the occasion, thereafter had a difficult relationship with the Emperor who had him brought by force to Fontainbleau to sign a concordat.

David captured the Emperor at the moment when, after crowning himself, he was about to crown Josephine, on December 2, 1804, in the cathedral of Notre-Dame de Paris. The generals, marshals and various other imperial figures are easily identifiable in this immense portrait gallery, which is strikingly vivid, despite its size.

One can recognize Pauline, Napoleon's favorite sister, and his mother, who in fact did not attend the ceremony. It is said that David, the high priest of neoclassicism, preferred the second version of his work.

The second monumental painting presents the army taking the oath when the flags were distributed to the regiment colonels, three years after the coronation. All the important civilian and political personalities of the time had gathered together for this ceremony on the Champs de Mars. Josephine, who was shown among them, was erased from the painting before its was shown at the Painting Salon of 1810, a year after she was repudiated. When the Emperor commissioned these two works, the painter was already famous for his *Oath of the Horatii* and *Oath of the Jeu de Paume*.

Other paintings on a smaller scale depict young Bonaparte or the Emperor, whereas between the arched windows, his two wives, Josephine and Marie-Louise, are shown in medallions.

From 1676 to 1682, this room was the upper part of the third chapel at Versailles. Here, in 1732, 1771 and 1787, King Louis XV and King Louis XVI called a meeting of the Parliament.

The Emperor's mark

Oddly enough, while many rooms were being continually remodeled, there remained one immense, barely decorated room, which was large enough to hold the Parliament when it was convened there. It proved to be exactly the room Louis-Philippe needed, almost naturally ready to receive this gigantic painting. On the right, Talleyrand is shown in profile, with a high and mighty, ironic look on his face, in contrast to the tense expressions of those around him. In this painting, which is the original and now hanging in the Louvre, David employed a stronger tone than in the second version, which incidentally he preferred.

The Hall of Battles

In 1837, this gallery with its imposing proportions (394 feet long and 43 feet wide) was devoted by Louis-Philippe to "princes of royal blood, admirals, constables, marshals of France and famous warriors killed in fighting for France." It replaced the Princes' Apartments on the first floor of the South Wing, which had been occupied by Monsieur, the brother of Louis XIV, and his wife La Palatine, then by the Duc de Chartres, the son of the Regent, the Dauphin, the Comte d'Artois and Madame Elizabeth.

The tribute in the form of busts and huge paintings is fitting in this solemn setting, designed by Fontaine and Nepveu in the style of the grand gallery of the Louvre. Monumental columns of gray marble holding up the entablatures suggest a temple. In the center of the ceiling, a cupola lights up the barrel vaulting ornamented with carved caissons, whereas around the room, large bronze plaques bear the names of people "killed in fighting for France." Most of these works were made by prestigious artists commissioned by Louis-Philippe. All the decisive battles in French history are commemorated here, from Tolbiac (496) when Clovis defeated the Alamans to Napoleon's

victories. Thirty-three scenes relate fourteen centuries of history, particularly *Bouvines, Fontenoy, Iena* and *Friedland,* painted by Horace Vernet and *Taillebourg* by Delacroix.

No doubt Louis-Philippe, who financed the museum with his own money, was moved by more than a desire to mark his reign by a spectacular action. In the back of his mind, he had the idea of gathering together in a single gesture of patriotic fervor clans that had been in conflict for fifty years. Here, those who were nostalgic for the Old Regime found a setting that some had known in their youth, whereas the soldiers of the old guard of Napoleon would be moved by the many paintings evoking the Emperor while others could rejoice in seeing dedicated "to all the glories of France" a place that had once been the showcase for only one of them.

Not everyone shared the same opinion about the museum. Balzac considered it "horribly bourgeois," while Victor Hugo declared: "Louis XIV has offered France a beautiful book, and you, Sire, have given it a magnificent binding." In any event, the remodeled area soon became a frequent choice for promenades of Parisians as well as residents of Versailles.

A museum of history

The Comte de Laborde wrote a fascinating book in 1848 on the occasion of the restoration of Versailles called Versailles ancien et moderne. *Here is what he had to say about Louis-Philippe:*

"He decided to devote the first floor of an entire wing of the palace to a gallery about three times larger than that of Louis XIV, and decorate it with thirty-three paintings representing the most celebrated actions of our history, a summary, as it were, of everything the palace contains, and to place in it the busts of eight warriors who died in the fighting (…)."

The second floor

The Small Private Apartments

Out of personal taste as well as following a fashion that had begun during the Regency, Louis XV continued throughout his life to have small rooms decorated at Versailles, where he could be alone or enjoy the company of his friends and mistresses. Even more than the Inner Apartments on the first floor, the private domain of Louis XV, where the King could give way to the man, was the suite of "rat's nests" he fitted out for himself on the second floor.

The second-floor rooms underwent constant renovation over time, both in their arrangement and their purpose. Today, there remain examples of what were once the apartments of Madame de Pompadour, Madame du Barry and the ministers of Louis XVI, Villequier and Maurepas. Simple staircases lead up to the floor, where corridors, cabinets, libraries, dining rooms, kitchens and workshops run into each other, and are distributed around the Marble Courtyard, the Deer Courtyard and the King's Small Courtyard. Louis XV had several of these rooms set aside as "his towers" where he enjoyed worked with wood and ivory. Several others were for books and maps, which he spent hours studying. He was fascinated by the expeditions to Lapland and Peru during the 1740s; they provided an opportunity to consolidate the theories of Newton about universal attraction, which Voltaire put into verse.

The progress of science as well as technology was a constant source of interest for Louis XV. His libraries (like those of his grandson, Louis XVI later on), contained more works of science than of literature.

The architects and decorators of the 18th century created a new style for these small rooms with low ceilings. The wood paneling and the furniture were carved more delicately, since they were closer to the eye and the limited size inspired cabinetmakers to design lighter furniture. As bathrooms became more numerous, vanity tables and daybeds were created. Consoles, chiffoniers, mechanical secretary desks and even chests of drawers were less cumbersome. The décor gained in refinement whatever it lost in majesty. It was a new way of being which indicated changes in society.

Louis XV received only a select group in his dining room on the second floor, including the Duc de Croÿ, the Prince de Soubise or the Maréchal de Saxe. Sometimes the King prepared the dishes himself and served his guests, sending the servants away as soon as the table was ready. For this purpose, he needed small pieces of furniture close at hand, where he could put bottles and accessories. Despite the intimate groups that met in the Small Apartments, they were decorated with extreme care. Verberckt carved magnificent wood panels and a varnish was developed to allow the walls to be colored in delicate pastel shades.

In the 18th century, there was an explosion of progress in every field, under the watchful eye of the philosophers. The early part of the century, which was dominated by rationalism, as well as the second half, when pre-Romanticism was born, were both periods during which France enjoyed outstanding influence.

European Courts followed the models of French painters, musicians, architects and men of letters. Frederick II of Prussia called Voltaire to his court at a time when diplomatic relations with Paris were very strained. French was understood in all the Courts and being able to speak it was a sign of cultivation. In return, artists and writers were immensely open to the world. The curiosity about exoticism, which had already begun developing at the end of the 17th century, caught on and became widespread. Boucher painted chinoiseries, while the public became passionately interested in the first-hand accounts of missionaries from the Far East who published their *Edifying and Curious Letters*.

Another passion, this time for building, took hold among the aristocrats, and even the King himself. Many of the *hotels particuliers* that continue to make Paris beautiful date from this period. A great deal of construction took place in Versailles as well: private mansions, and also extensions of the chateau, such as the

Post Office, the War Office and the Foreign Affairs Office. At the end of her life, Madame de Pompadour had an Ursuline convent built which Mique completed after her death. Today, it is the Lycée Hoche, and is considered one of the most beautiful vestiges in the town. To imagine what it was like to live in an aristocratic home at the time, the Lambinet Museum (which was also built under Louis XV) offers magnificent reconstructions of period furnishings.

The look of the towns and daily life changed radically, due to designs that all tended in the same direction: to achieve happiness on earth. In their paintings of romantic feasts, Watteau and Fragonard transcribed the atmosphere of these years, when the

perfection. Madame de Pompadour had the manufacture which was initially set up in Vincennes moved to Sèvres, and in 1760, she made it a Royal Manufacture. Porcelain pieces were present everywhere in the rooms she occupied.

Louis XV considerably increased the living space of Madame de Pompadour compared to the rather reduced apartment given to the first resident on the second floor, Madame de Mailly. The King had a room prepared for Madame de Pompadour at the beginning of their liaison. She reigned for five years on the second floor, above the Salon of War, before moving down to settle on the ground floor. Later on, Madame du Barry was to have a six-room suite.

aristocracy devoted itself to the search for lighthearted amusement, wit and the joy of living.

Although Voltaire paid homage to the century of Louis XIV: "Genius has only one century, after which it must degenerate," the reign of Louis XV certainly matched it in terms of personal fulfillment. Voltaire implicitly acknowledged as much when he said of his own period: "Oh! What a good time is this age of iron." In the 18th century, porcelain also reached a peak of

The era of favorites ended with Louis XVI. After Madame du Barry was sent into exile, the King's "favorites" were replaced by the Duc de Villequier and the Comte de Maurepas, who was disgraced by Louis XV for his hostility towards Madame de Pompadour and called back to the Court by Louis XVI when he took the throne. The rest of the second floor was again turned into a place of study, where Louis XVI liked to withdraw to enjoy his hobbies.

Madame du Barry's library

Typical of the intimate rooms that appeared in the 18th century in all aristocratic and royal homes, this library suggests a new art of living. The porcelain flowers that are barely visible on the right decorate a birdcage, recalling the fashion among courtiers for birds and parrots.

The Chapel

The roof of the chapel dominates at a right angle to the main building when one approaches the château from the Parade Ground. The chapel was always one of the most important places in the life of the Court. Aside from daily Mass and religious feast days, births, baptisms and royal marriages were celebrated there, as well as political events such as victories and peace treaties. Like all the other activities at Versailles, these ceremonies were the occasion for displays of splendor and jostling crowds as the King passed by. Dedicated by Louis XIV to Saint-Louis, the chapel was designed as much as a hymn to the royal household as for divine worship. After the death of Louis XIV, Louis XV and Louis XVI and the important families of Versailles prayed there as well, calling upon Saint Anne, Saint Marie, Saint Thérèse and Saint Adélaïde, all names of members of the royal family.

"There is no place in Versailles that hasn't been remodeled ten times," Princess Palatine used to say, and indeed, four other chapels preceded this one. It was begun in 1700 by Mansart and completed by Robert de Cotte ten years later, only five years before the end of the reign of Louis XIV. This explains the relatively modern look of the edifice and many of those who worked on it were indeed called in on projects for Louis XV later on. In the vestibule on the first floor, all of the decoration, except for the colored marble floor, consists of white stone sculptures, columns and medallions, which give it a rather sober appearance. When the King walked through the gilded doors, he found himself in the gallery of the chapel, built on the classical plan of a palatine chapels with two floors. The large windows that bring in daylight and the white stone of the walls and the tall Corinthian columns bathe the entire chapel in impressive luminosity.

The Royal Chapel

The chapel, a splendid marble vessel 144 feet long and 82 feet high, is the fifth one since the château was first built. The magnificent organ case is found in an unusual place, above the high altar, because of the royal gallery.

The opulent decorations, which are rich and colorful, contrast with the simplicity of the stone: the floor covered with colored marble, the vault painted by Coypel, paintings by Lemoyne and Lafosse, sculptures by Nicolas and Guillaume Coustou and Le Pautre, all of them generously enlivened by gold or gilt bronze.

Although Voltaire mockingly claimed it was "an astonishing bauble," the chapel is actually a remarkable example of 18th liturgical art, particularly the sculpture. No doubt the "Very Christian King" wanted the chapel to display the importance he attached to the faith, especially the Catholic faith, which he had tried to impose throughout his life. The high altar with its bas-relief by Van Clève and the organ case by Cliquot, the greatest craftsman of his time, are the principal showpieces.

Mass was said every day at ten o'clock or at midday, depending on the time of year, with the Queen seated to the right of her husband, the ladies in the gallery and the courtiers on the ground floor in the nave, all of them turned towards the King. The music, for which Louis XIV, like his father, showed genuine appreciation, played an important role in these ceremonies. Delalande, Couperin and Charpentier played their most beautiful works for Versailles. Monarchy, devotion and splendor were closely linked at Versailles. When Louis XV laid the cornerstone for a new church near the castle (now Saint-Louis Cathedral) in 1734, he used a silver trowel. In his efforts to make the chateau more comfortable, he had small, sumptuously decorated niches put into the galleries. In winter, he and a few privileged persons (including Madame de Pompadour) could follow the Mass sheltered from the cold.

Some of the great names of the Church were connected to the sovereigns at Versailles, such as Bourdaloue, Father La Chaise and Bossuet. A pupil of Saint Vincent de Paul, and former preceptor of the Dauphin, Bossuet was appointed Bishop of Meaux in 1681, but frequently came back to the Court as the Dauphine's chaplain. Bossuet was known for his unusual eloquence, but he was more than an orator. In 1675, he dared to remind the King that taxes were crushing the already poverty-stricken peasants: "You should consider, Sire, that the throne you occupy belongs to God, and that you are taking His place, and that you must reign according to His laws."

The Royal Opera

The harmony of blue and pink and the refinement of the decorations evoke the grace and preciousness of paintings by Boucher, Watteau and Fragonard. It is easy to imagine a gala evening in the 18th century in this setting. The generous gilding and sparkle of the chandeliers blended with the rich fabrics of Court dress and the gems of their adornment. Luxury, which ruled here, was nevertheless different from that in the Hall of Mirrors. Like the chapel, which linked the reign of Louis XIV to that of Louis XV, the Royal Opera linked the reign of Louis XV to that of Louis XVI. There is a clarity and freshness in its richness similar to the atmosphere of the Trianons. Here, the rococo style is so delicate that it is not weighed down even by the profusion of details.

This masterpiece by Jacques Ange Gabriel was completed with amazing celerity in just twenty-one months, from 1768 to 1770, though it was preceded by numerous experiments and abandoned projects. Louis XIII and Louis XIV were passionately interested in music, which was present everywhere, yet no particular place at the palace was reserved for it during their reigns. It was not until the end of the reign of Louis XV that it was finally given an official setting. Until then, temporary stages and stage settings were mounted for specific occasions. Performances were put on in the gardens, the ring at the Royal Stables (where the musicians were housed), the Small Gallery (destroyed in 1769) for which Madame de Pompadour has a particular liking, the Great Cabinet and the Ambassadors' Staircase.

Under Louis XIV, a hall was set up for a time between the Princes' Courtyard and the Passage du Midi, where the Court was entertained by great names such as Lully and Delalande. The sovereign planned to build a permanent opera house and put Vigarani, who built the machinery for the theatre in Fontainebleau, in charge of the design. Construction work began in 1685, but with little enthusiasm, and was halted three years later by the war of the League of Augsburg.

Louis XV in turn revived the project. Jacques Ange Gabriel, his architect, drew up plans in 1748 but they did not materialize any more than the previous ones. In 1763, he presented new ones, but once again, the building proceeded at a dull pace, due perhaps at least in part, to the fact that Gabriel was seventy years old, a venerable age at the time. In the end, it took the prospect of the Dauphin's wedding to precipitate the work. Two men provided the King with active, talented support at the time: Pajou, who directed the team of sixteen sculptors, and Arnoult, who had designed the movable floor system at Fontainebleau. The work progressed well, and once again, Versailles had a gigantic worksite employing up to two hundred and fifty masons.

The ellipse-shaped hall was covered in wood painted to imitate marble. No doubt there were several reasons for this choice: it was economical, fast and improved the acoustics. Arnoult's machinery made it possible to raise the orchestra to the level of the stage, to create a huge banquet hall. In May 1770, the barely finished Royal Opera served as a setting for the "Royal Feast" celebrating the marriage of the future Louis XVI and the Archduchess of Austria, Marie-Antoinette. For several days of festivities, Versailles was adorned with all its famous pomp, including gold dishes on the banquet table, adding to the enchantment of the décor. A special hall was set up for the occasion to house eighty orchestra musicians.

A few days later, Lully's *Persée* was presented, then a Costume Ball at which the Dauphin and his bride danced their first minuet. A salon with harmonious blue and gold decoration, heightened by mirrors, had been added to the stage. The performances that followed were no less prestigious: Racine's *Athalie* and Voltaire's *Tancrède*, along with a number of ballets when horses were sometimes brought on stage.

While spectators marveled at the festivities, the *Intendant des Menus Plaisirs* (Steward of Small

Gabriel's masterpiece

Curiously, in spite of the importance attached to lyric opera by the Court, it was not until the wedding of the Dauphin and Marie-Antoinette that Louis XV ordered Gabriel to build the Royal Opera, which had been in the planning stages for twenty years. In just twenty months, Gabriel produced a masterpiece of blue, pink and gold wood that looked like marble. He designed the first oval hall in France, which was the country's largest theatre until the Paris Opera was built a century later. The orchestra, the balcony and two floors of boxes seated 700 people and a third could be added.

Pleasures), also known by the charming name of "Butterfly of the Fortress," was soon worried. The costumes, performers and musicians, as well as lighting, which required three thousand candles, were swallowing up alarming sums of money. Consequently, such luxurious entertainment was limited to exceptional occasions, especially to honor visitors. Josef II, Marie Antoinette's brother, was able to attend a performance of Rameau's *Castor et Pollux* and Gustav III was treated to Gluck's *Armide* in 1784. The Queen's interest in music (she herself played the harpsichord and the harp) was an advantage for Gluck in his quarrel with Piccinni.

The Royal Opera was also the setting for the wedding of the Comte de Provence (the future Louis XVIII) and that of the Comte d'Artois (the future Charles X), and during the Second Empire, the state visit of Queen Victoria. It suffered some deterioration, like many other rooms in the palace, at the end of the 19th century, when someone had the unfortunate idea of installing a glass roof. During the major restoration undertaken in 1952, the original ceiling was reconstructed and adorned with a painting by Durumeau. When Queen Elizabeth II came to visit in 1957, she was able to see the Royal Opera in the splendid condition it had enjoyed two centuries earlier.

GARDENS AND TRIANONS

Flowerbeds and fountains

Hercules

The gardens, like the apartments, were peopled with mythological subjects. Here, it was not the great deeds of the King but rather the hours, seasons and natural elements that were magnified under the features of the Olympian gods. Each fountain and statue evokes an episode from ancient myths. Here, Hercules stands daydreaming, leaning on his club and contemplating the skin of the lion of Nemea, which he has just choked with his bare hands. The hero shall meditate for eternity: having skinned the lion, he realized that nothing could pierce it, and he was able to tear it only with the lion's claws.

"One should come to Versailles on a bright autumn day," said Pierre de Nolhac. Voltaire, Anna de Noailles and Victor Hugo, among so many famous visitors, were charmed by the admirable gardens which some see as a luxurious setting and others as nature guided by the hand of artists.

Each season presents a radically different side of this royally ordered nature. When one evokes Venice in winter, it is to call attention to its unexpected beauty and the incongruity of the ice-covered Grand Canal and the Piazza San Marco silent but for the wings of the pigeons. The gardens of Versailles, though less frequently praised as the apotheosis of winter splendor, have no cause to be jealous of their neighbor across the Alps.

The gardens stand outside of time, cut off from the noises and concerns of ordinary life, revealing a facet of eternity. It might well be three centuries earlier without changing a single detail: the same still basins, the splendid golden nymphs emerging from the water, the silhouette of the sunlit branches against the sky, and the song of a few birds that lost their way south. Versailles appears to be a timeless dwelling offered up to the calm beauty of the walls and the nymphs.

Then spring arrives, with a rustling in the flowerbeds, the buds, the fountain animals, the birds and the branches. Every year, Versailles recreates the spectacle of nature's amazing youth. The warmth of summer makes the evenings heavy and sultry, and one can easily imagine the sound of stifled laughter coming from every grove, where young women in dresses with panniers keep secret rendezvous with idle courtiers.

Then, in autumn, nature rejoices at Versailles, letting loose the rich palette of glorious earth colors.

The first festivities at Versailles took place in the greenery of the gardens. At the time, the walls of the castle had not yet been decorated with marble and gold; even the groves had to be covered with painted canvas to hide the construction work under way or to imitate statues that had not yet joined their bases. Nevertheless, *The Way to Present the Gardens of Versailles,* which Louis XIV wrote in about 1690, testifies to his enthusiasm. He noted every point of interest, from the Steps of Latona to the Trianon in the woods: "One should pause to take in the sprays of Neptune and the Sea Monster," "one should point out the bas-relief," "one should draw attention to the variety of fountains," etc. Though he did not add any commentary, the profusion of detail in the inventory reveals the pride of its author.

The King enjoyed a special complicity with Le Nôtre, to which Dangerau attests in his Journal: "The King liked to see him and talk with him (…). (Louis XIV) had him put in a wheelchair like his own. He took him on a tour of all the gardens and Mr. Le Nôtre said," Oh, my poor father, if you were only alive today and could see me, a poor gardener, being promenaded next to the greatest king in the world (…)."

The Parterre du Midi

Two parterres or flowerbeds frame the Parterre d'Eau or ornamental pool in the center of the terrace. In his essay The Way to Present the Gardens of Versailles, *Louis XIV advised: "One should stop at the top of the steps [of Latona] to look at the arrangement of the flowerbeds, the ornamental pools and the fountains of the Cabinets (…). Then, one should turn left (…). One should pause to look at the Parterre du Midi." This flowerbed stretched out beneath the windows of the Queen's Apartments. On the left, one can see the Vase of Peace and below, the Salon of Peace.*

When Louis XIV conferred a title of nobility upon Le Nôtre in 1675, the latter modestly requested that three snails be include on his coat of arms. The "poor gardener" who "couldn't stand short vistas" gave the chateau not just an extension, but an inseparable complement to its beauty and charm. He was already well known when Louis XIV entrusted the Versailles gardens to him. He was the son of the first gardener of the Tuileries, and he himself had been gardener to the King for fifteen years. He produced the gardens of Vaux-

le-Vicomte for Fouquet, and he reached the height of his art for Louis XIV as he approached the age of fifty.

Since Louis XIV was creating a new palace out of his father's original one, he enlarged and embellished the gardens and preserved some of the earlier lines drawn by the gardeners of Louis XIII. Jacques de Nemours, Mollet, Masson and Claude Denis also designed flowerbeds adorned with fountains that were supplied with water by a pump installed in

Clagny Pond. The Tapis Vert (the Green Rug), also known as the King's Walk, was planned, ending in a "rondeau of swans" which became the Fountain of Apollo. From this sketch, Le Nôtre created the model for the French-style garden.

The gardens were given the same ornamental treatment as the buildings: long vistas, symmetrical pathways enlivened by statues, vases and groves, flowerbeds reproducing the swirls of the palace decorations and water, present everywhere, mirroring the light and stone. The gardeners used one hundred and fifty thousand plants to create the North, South and Latona flowerbeds. The plants were replaced up to fifteen times a year to keep the colors from fading.

Le Brun often helped in designing the floral patterns, as well as the statues adorning the gardens and fountains, while J. Hardouin-Mansart took part in planning the whole complex.

The Gardens of Le Nôtre

"There was a marsh and there were architects and gardeners. And there were angles, triangles, rectangles, circles and pyramids. And there was a garden and this garden lived with the soul of Le Nôtre." This is how Cocteau described the French-style garden whose geometrical lines are obvious here.

Next pages

The Tapis Vert

The gardens of Versailles were planned around this central axis, also known as the King's Walk or the Solar Axis, from the very beginning of the chateau under Louis XIII. From the Parterre of Latona to the Fountain of Apollo (seen from the back), a profusion of statues and vases were used to decorate the gardens.

Pages 88-89

The Baths of Apollo

The first grotto, built up against the chateau, held the statues of Thetis and Phebus-Apollo. It disappeared during the palace extension, and its décor went through a number of episodes until Hubert Robert reconstructed the grotto. In the center, Apollo, surrounded by nymphs, is received by Thetis, the mother of all rivers, in her underwater grotto. On either side, Tritons dress the wounds of his horses. La Fontaine clearly assimilates the sun-god to the sovereign in Les Amours de Psyche:

"When the sun is weary and has finished his task, He descends to the home of Thetis, to take his rest."

Pages 92-93

The Fountain of Autumn

The Marsy brothers sculpted this Bacchus surrounded by four satyrs, based on a drawing by Le Brun, in about 1673. The mysterious smile on the lips of the wine god is worthy of a painting by Leonardo da Vinci.

It took the folly of a King and the genius of Le Nôtre to succeed in creating such as astonishing osmosis, especially as the site did not lend itself to the project. The land, which abounded in game, was more suitable to hunters than builders. Extraordinary ingenuity and enormous efforts were required to transform the steep, marshy surroundings of the chateau into a wide terrace that sloped gently downwards.

During the works, in which the army often took partmany workers suffered from fever. For a long time, courtiers at Versailles complained of breathing fetid air. Accidents occurredfrequently and sometimes they were fatal. The meticulous accounts kept by Colbert include the number of pensions attributed to widows, along with a table of compensation drawn up for the injuries sustained. More and more fountains were built, which created a new problem. The water supplied by the pump at Clagny, built by the Francini brothers, whose ancestors had already been hydraulic engineers at Saint-Germain under Henri IV, was no longer sufficient. Louis XIV decided to embark on a mad enterprise.

First, a pump was built at Marly on an arm of the Seine, between Bougival and Croissy, to transport water by aqueduct to Versailles. Then, a plan was devised to divert water from the Eure River, but the ruinous project was abandoned at the beginning of the war of the League of Augsburg. The "Full Play of the Fountains", which was inaugurated in 1660, is now reserved for special occasions.

In May 1664, however, there was no question of restrictions when Louis XIV held the memorable feast called "Pleasures of the Enchanted Island" to please his mistress Louise de La Vallière. The King's reign had just begun and he was still a young man who found Molière amusing. Molière's troupe, the Actors of Monsieur, the King's brother, had already taken part in the festivities at Vaux-le-Vicomte. In a single week, Molière had written and presented *l'Impromptu de Versailles* before the King, and the ten days of the "Enchanted Island" offered even greater honors. After a performance of *Rolando Furioso* with the King in the leading role, Molière and his actors took part in a parade in which he played the god Pan, perched atop a machine invented by Vigarani. The next day, he staged a play outdoors, *La Princesse d'Elide*, accompanied by Lully's musicians.

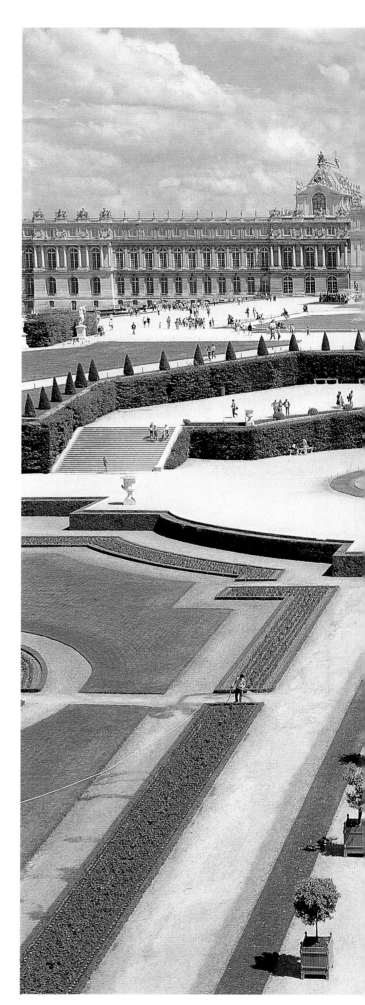

The King's heart is won over in the first scene:
"When love offers your eyes a pleasant choice,
Surrender to your ardor, young beauties,
For, at an age when one is most lovable,
Nothing is more beautiful than loving.

The invitation could not help but touch the young sovereign enamored by young Louise. Molière also performed *Les Fâcheux* (written for Vaux-le-Vicomte), and then, in the Marble Courtyard, the first three acts of *Tartuffe* which at first was given a cool reception, and later aroused angry opposition. In his preface to the 1669 edition, Molière wrote: "The marquis, the *precieuses,* the cuckolds and the doctors quietly suffered at seeing themselves represented (…) but the hypocrites heard no mockery, who piously curse and damn me with charity (…)." Finally, *Le Mariage forcé* brought smiles back to everyone's faces. The ten days of performances, interspersed with fireworks, splendid banquets, games and concerts, marked the

beginning of a new era: they definitively surpassed the painful memory of Vaux-le-Vicomte and made the loves of Louis XIV and of Versailles official. Again, Colbert sighed: "Oh, what a pity, that the greatest of kings should be measured against Versailles."

Other festivities took place in this setting. When the Grand Canal was dug, the Republic of Venice offered gondoliers and gondolas to the Sun King. At evening celebrations, they could be seen, lit up and filled with musicians, going back and forth on the waters of the Grand Canal all the way to the Trianon. The King loved to go to his favorite residence by water. He added his own fleet to the gondolas: two small sailboats, nine rowboats decorated by Caffieri, two yachts from England and a galley.

The embarkation site, near the Fountain of Apollo, still bears the name "Little Venice," and the neighboring woods the "Sailors' Woods."

The Fountain of Latona

J. Hardouin-Mansart changed this ornamental pool in 1689 to make it more spectacular. Situated at the foot of the steps leading to the Parterre d'Eau and in line with the Tapis Vert, he wanted the fountain to be sumptuous. From the gilded lead subjects adorning the basin (frogs and people undergoing metamorphosis) gush some fifty fountains. At the top, Diana and Apollo stand on either side of their mother, Latona. The goddess had once wished to bathe her children in a spring, but was prevented from doing so by shepherds. Fearsome mother that she was, Latona turned the troublesome shepherds into frogs.

In 1668, Louis XIV offered the Court "The Great Royal Entertainment" and there was further country merrymaking in 1674 to celebrate the first lengthy stay in Versailles. These evening feasts, for which Vigarani designed painted cardboard decors lit up by myriad candles and fireworks, can still make us dream, thanks to the engravings by Israel Silvestre. In addition to these privileged moments, Louis XIV visited the gardens he deeply loved every day, on foot or by sedan chair, surrounded by a few people he wished to distinguish. "Madame de La Fayette was at Versailles yesterday, " recounts a contemporary. "The King had her ride in the coach with the ladies and took pleasure in showing her the beauty of Versailles, like an ordinary person one visits at his country home."

The promenades sometimes ended with a small collation enjoyed in a grassy spot, with the King's musicians playing in the background. Some winters, the gardens offered other charms. The frozen Grand Canal was filled with sleighs and the snow-covered grass turned into playing fields. Near the Swiss ornamental pool, a vegetable garden was planted, which is still tended today by the National School of Horticulture. La Quintinie worked for seven years to bring the immense plot to bear the particular fruits and vegetables of which the King was especially fond: asparagus, melon and peas, which were creating a "sensation" at the time, according to Madame de Sévigné. The orchard was the agronomist's pride and job, where he cultivated three hundred varieties of pear. It soon became one of the favorite spots of Louis XIV.

Around the "Small Garden" which included the Trianon and the Grand Canal, the estate comprised fifteen thousand acres of woods, reserved for hunting. A fence marked the passage from one to the other. The "Grand Garden", which was completely surrounded by a wall, was dismantled during the Revolution.

The Fountain of Diana

Apollo's twin sister, Diana, appears almost as often as her brother in the décor of Versailles. Here, the huntress, brandishing her bow towards the setting sun, was sculpted by Desjardins. Diana, who personified the Moon in the ancient world, symbolizes the Evening Hour.

Apollo's Chariot

Louis XIV had this fountain built at the site of the "rondeau of the swans", created under Louis XIII. This sculpture group, made of gilded lead by Tuby, is one of the most gripping at Versailles: four powerful horses are pulling the chariot of the sun out of the waters, after leaving the grotto of Thetis.

The Fountain of Apollo

The gardens of Versailles were designed so that the surrounding town would never be visible. Thus, from the Fountain of Apollo, one has an unobstructed view to the far end of the Tapis Vert to the east and the long arm of the Grand Canal to the west. Le Nôtre, who loved "unlimited vistas" succeeded in creating a most grandiose view.

The Winter Fountain

The Winter sculpture group was made by Girardon. The old man, Winter, assimilated here with Saturn, is surrounded by cherubs, in keeping with the desire of Louis XIV, who wanted to see "childhood" everywhere. The fountains of the four seasons punctuate the two main walkways parallel to the Tapis Vert. Autumn and Winter to the south, and Spring and Summer to the north.

When Louis XV returned to Versailles, he was determined to keep up the work of his great-grandfather, despite heavy maintenance costs.

During his reign, the gardens nevertheless underwent a major transformation. The arbors along the pathways vanished, due to age and harsh winters. In losing the arbors and the fences that structured them, the garden lost some of its architectural appearance. Similarly, of the "grassy cabinets," "ballrooms" and "concert halls," only the names remained. Bit by bit, the light constructions scattered throughout the gardens disappeared. Visitors caused extensive damage to the plants and flowerbeds and, at one point, Louis XV prohibited access to outsiders. The measure aroused such furor that he soon relented: the public considered Versailles a public "good."

At the beginning of his reign, Louis XVI decided to replace the hundred-year-old trees. The paintings of Hubert Robert bear testimony to the gigantic project undertaken from 1774 to 1775. The Sun King's descendent made only one concession to the new fashion of "English-style" gardens, and that was to the Queen. Otherwise, he insisted that "everything be put back as it should be."

Three centuries later, the layout of the estate Louis XIV once took such pleasure in showing his guests looks more or less the same. Though the area of "Small Garden" has been cut in half, it still covers 1,500 acres including 250 acres of flower gardens. From the main building of the chateau, the terraced garden descends a slope of 105 feet from the Parterre d'Eau to the Grand Canal. From every angle, the visitor's gaze is lost in the expanse of the gardens or the palace that dominates them.

The Tapis Vert, which is extended by the long Grand Canal, divides the gardens in two massive parts, to the east and the west. Fountains are spaced out in its axis, from the ornamental pools at the foot of the castle, to the Fountain of Latona, 33 feet below, then to the Fountain of Apollo at the end of the King's Walk. Two hundred statues, cherubs and cupids, vases and statues on pedestals decorate the space, in keeping with the wishes of Louis XIV. In foundries and sculpture studios, the greatest artists of the age crafted these works, often from drawings by Le Brun. Among the most famous, the Marsy brothers, Coysevox, Girardon, Tuby, Regnaudin, Hardy and Bouchardin sometimes worked together to produce this huge, open-air museum.

The Orangery

If one follows the advice of Louis XIV, one should arrive at the Orangery from the South Parterre, which overlooks it. Louis XIV expressed his concern in a letter to Colbert from his camp in Besançon: "Send news of the effect produced by the orange trees in their appointed place." Upon his return, he was so proud of the results that he immediately ordered a series of engravings to immortalize them.

During his reign, 2,000 orange trees in tubs were mixed with myrtle, oleander and pomegranate trees to form an "exotic" oasis which the King found enchanting. Since then, date trees have been added, but the esplanade now has only about 1,200 bushes.

Le Vau built an initial Orangery, which was soon judged to be too small. Starting in 1678, earthworks were begun to enlarge the area for a new Orangery.

Louis XIV placed Hardouin-Mansart in charge of drawing up the plans, including a long gallery, dug beneath the parterre, and two others under the Stairway of the Hundred Steps, on either side of the grass and the central basin.

Today, as in the time of the Kings, daylight streams through high, arched windows into the galleries where the trees and plants are kept during the winter.

The Orangery was filled with the fragrance of the myriad essences housed there, which made it a choice setting for feasts and military parades. It was difficult to keep up, however, as the engineers were often bothered by water leaking into the gallery and the necessary repairs called for heavy expenditures.

The Swiss Guard have left their name to the neighboring ornamental pool, which they spent considerable effort digging out of marshy land between 1678 and 1682. The edges of this huge lake, at the foot of the Satory Woods, immediately became a favorite place for promenades among the residents of Versailles who wanted to escape from the crowded garden walks.

A whiff of exoticism

Situated between the South Parterre and the long Swiss ornamental pool, the Orangery offers plants that are as unusual as they are appealing. Louis XIV showed a lively interest in his orange trees, but it was Louis XV, above all, who developed the fashion for tropical products, materialized especially by "chinoiseries."

The Grand Trianon

From the very beginning of the works to enlarge Versailles, the King had a new edifice built at the far end of the gardens. By 1668, the estate had expanded in the northwest to include a village named Trianon. Two years later, Le Vau had it razed to build a one-storey pavilion where Louis came for light meals in the company of Madame de Montespan. "It appears that Louis XIV wished immediately to replace the small chateau now disappearing, which was a place for feasting and the pleasures of youth," commented Pierre de Nolhac.

In this spot, devoted solely to pleasure, the decoration was in no way pompous, but rather combined gaiety with exuberance. All the rooms were blue and white, matching the color of the glazed tiles from Delft, Nevers and Rouen that covered the inside and outside walls. Even the furniture, with its refined, extravagant shapes, was varnished in the same tones, along with the benches in the surrounding garden. The roofs and balustrades were decorated with porcelain vases featuring floral and bird motifs.

Louis XIV wanted an exceptional garden for his retreat. Using a series of greenhouses, he had it planted with orange trees, tuberoses and jasmine, as well as rare essences that were collected in a "perfume cabinet." The King liked strong fragrances. The fragile Porcelain Trianon, in its floral setting, did not survive the grace of the Marquise. By 1687, it was very deteriorated and was demolished. The little pavilion, "extraordinary and convenient for spending a few hours of the day during the summer heat," according to Félibien, gave way to the marble Trianon, this time built in honor of Madame de Maintenon. The latter was no longer interested in entertainment, however, and eventually, she even had the theatre in the Trianon destroyed.

Jules Hardouin-Mansart and Le Nôtre worked together on this construction which the King's impatience made an arduous task. Harassed by the sovereign, Louvois noted that the King's visits to the work site increased, along with ensuing stormy discussions. The King could not stand being deprived of his favorite abode.

A pink marble palace

Saint-Simon sums up quite well the stages in the life of this pavilion, originally built for Madame de Montespan: "Trianon: first a porcelain house for light meals, then enlarged to be able to sleep there, and finally, a marble palace." After Madame de Maintenon, Madame de Pompadour and Madame du Barry, the Empress Josephine liked to stay here in the company of the Emperor, who preferred the Trianon to the chateau itself.

Saint-Simon reported on one of the confrontations between Louvois and the sovereign. Louis XIV had noticed a flaw in the proportions of a window, and his Superintendent refused to admit it. The King, said Saint-Simon, had "a compass in his eye for accuracy and symmetry" and when the window was measured, the monarch was proved right. Finally, Louis XIV gave an inaugural dinner there in January 1688, in a still unfinished setting, since the new palace would not be furnished until the end of that year. The King immediately began organising promenades, concerts and plays for his inner circle.

of the courtiers who watched every move he made in the palace. The building was gradually extended until it looked much as it does today, with long façades topped by Italian-style balustrades reminiscent of those on the chateau, yet punctuated everywhere by green Campan marble columns and pink Laguedoc marble pilasters.

Robert de Cotte gave the building one of its principal charms, the peristyle or open colonnade that links the two wings into a splendid complex. The space, opening onto the courtyard and the gardens, was often used as a summer dining room by Louis XIV. At the beginning of her reign, Marie Leszczynska liked to stay at the Trianon where she would entertain her father on his visits. Louis XV showed little interest in it until 1750, when Madame de Pompadour took her place as the official favorite.

The Marquise, who was not well-received by the Court, had absolute authority here to organize entertainment to amuse the sovereign. The rooms were redecorated for her in the "new fashion" of light silks and the latest furniture designs. The "Louis XV" style extended even to the gardens, which were adorned with trellises, and the flowerbeds were replanted.

The Grand Trianon was somewhat neglected under Louis XVI. As everyone knows, Marie-Antoinette preferred the small neighboring chateau and her hamlet. The marble Trianon was assigned to receiving guests visiting Versailles.

With the arrival of Napoleon, new renovation works were undertaken. He modified the size and decoration of the rooms.

They are fitted out mostly with the Directory or Empire-style furnishings he chose for them. The Malachite Room, the bedchamber and above all the Work Cabinet (which was Madame de Maintenon's bedchamber), are outstanding examples of the style. The green and gold wall hangings, the bowls and marble tables held up by caryatides, ebony furniture inlaid with bronze, often made by Jacob-Desmalter, testify to the Emperor's taste for munificence in furnishings.

"Never leave your affairs for your pleasure; but always make it a rule to give yourself time for freedom and entertainment," wrote Louis XIV to his grandson. Trianon was where the King enjoyed these entertainments, escaping for a few hours from the obligations of his position, under the constant gaze

The Bedchamber of the Empress

After the Revolution, Versailles underwent another period of transformation and glory during the Empire. This bedchamber belonged to Louis XIV; Napoleon had it restored for Marie-Louise..

Napoleon preferred this residence to the chateau itself. He wanted his mother to live there, and began renovation work in one of the wings for that purpose. Laetitia, who did not like the place, refused the apartments designed for her. Her son, on the contrary, enjoyed staying there with the Empress until Josephine was repudiated and relegated to Malmaison in 1809. The Emperor spent several days following the divorce at the Trianon, where one imagines him walking gloomily from one room to another. Two years later, he again resided here for a while with Marie-Louise de Hapsburg (the great-niece of Marie-Antoinette), who had become his wife in 1810. As in the days of royal celebrations, the Grand Canal was covered with boats filled with players and musicians, and the groves were illuminated for the crowds of spectators.

After twenty years of unrest during the events of the Restoration and fleeting appearances of Louis XVIII and Charles X, Louis-Philippe entrusted the renovation of the Trianon to the architect Nepveu. The citizen-king had a "family room" fitted out which still has its original décor. He lived there with the Queen, Marie-Amélie, surrounded by his five sons and daughters, including the eldest, Louise, who became the wife of Leopold I of Belgium in 1832. During this period, the Belgian sovereigns were often guests at the Trianon, where one of the rooms still carries their name.

Versailles became a fashionable town once again, with salons frequented by all the famous personalities of the time: Chopin and Liszt, Balzac, Georges Sand, Musset and Dumas père, mixed in with the literary lions and lionesses of the Saint-Louis district, the Avenue of Saint-Cloud and the Boulevard du Roi. The Montansier theatre also drew many Parisians, actors and spectators alike, such as Madame Récamier and Rachel, one of the greatest tragedians of the age.

Then came the Revolution of 1848, and the exile of the royal family. When Louis-Philippe left the Tuileries, he stopped at the Trianon to spend a few hours in solitude before continuing on his way to England. The Trianon then witnessed a series of guests during the Second Empire, and after the defeat

The Garden Room

This salon, situated at the end of the gallery, no doubt benefits the most from the advantages of the Trianon's ground-floor construction.

of Sedan, two other, less welcome guests, Bismark and the Emperor Wilhelm. The little palace was uninhabited under the republics that followed, and became increasingly deteriorated.

It was not until the 20th century that Pierre de Nolhac, a curator who cherished Versailles, finally put an end to the slow deterioration. After another long period of time, General de Gaulle decided to revive the restoration of the Trianon, which was completed in 1966. Today, the Trianon serves as a place for receiving guests whom the government wishes to honor in a special way, just as it did under the kings.

The Petit Trianon

If Versailles brings to mind the Sun King and the Grand Trianon the Emperor, the Petit Trianon, nestled among trees and meadows, remains permeated by the memory of Marie-Antoinette. Her spontaneity and tastes, reflecting the new art of living that developed in her time, seem to be embodied in this fresh setting. Yet, the initiative to build it came from Louis XV. "I made Versailles for the Court, Marly for my friends and Trianon for myself," said Louis XIV.

Similarly, Louis XV "made" the Petit Trianon to flee from the one his ancestor had built several decades earlier in his continual search for privacy. Before having the small castle constructed, Louis XV endeavoured to turn the domain into a center of agronomy. Starting in 1751, Claude Richard and Jussieu set up a botanical garden, which soon became renowned throughout Europe. Rare species, brought back from the four corners of the earth by the Royal Navy, were collected there, while Jussieu continued his research on diseases affecting wheat. Louis XV followed these experiments with passionate interest and constantly improved the facilities to allow the cultivation of pineapple, nettle and fig trees in the middle of Ile de France. The Chèvreloup Arboretum, adjoining the garden, still has among its magnificent specimens a *sophora japonica* planted during this reign. The King was so appreciative of this haven that he had a menagerie installed at the other end of the Grand Canal from 1949 to 1753. Except for the presence of a few sculptures, it was a genuine experimental farm, with its own dairy. Nothing is left today of "these floral, herb and vegetable gardens (…) spread out with a great deal of taste and which were extremely costly," according to the Duc de Croÿ.

The French Garden was created during the same period, along with the "French Pavilion" built by Gabriel in 1750, which has come down to us intact. The sober lines of this white stone pavilion prefigure the style of Louis XVI. The white and gold interior decoration recalls the building's rural setting with a cornice motif of frolicking roosters and swans and wood panelling by Verberckt.

Marie-Antoinette's theater

The queen was only twenty years old when the first theater performances were held for her at the Grand Trianon. Three years later, Mique presented a project, which he completed in less than two years. On the outside, it was a delicate building, hidden amid the greenery, not far from the Petit Trianon. Inside, it was a delightful theatre, inspired by the superb Opera designed by Gabriel for the chateau. To keep costs down, pasteboard was freely used, even for some sculptures. In this private domain, where Marie-Antoinette sometimes liked to perform on stage herself, only very close members of her family and a few select friends were allowed.

A few graceful ornamental pools decorated with cherubs give the surroundings the same simple charm and gaiety. Then, starting in 1762, Gabriel deployed his neo-classical style in building the Petit Trianon, located very close by. Madame de Pompadour, who instigated the project, did not live to see it completed. When it was finally inaugurated in 1768, she had been dead for four years.

The small, square, one-storey palace with an attic was built by Louis XV, who manifested the same careful attention that Louis XIV had shown for his own works. He selected wrought-iron motifs, ordered drawings of the edifice before it was completed and supervised the organisation of the surrounding gardens. Flowers were omnipresent, in garlands on the wood panelling, furniture and fireplaces.

Although Madame de Pompadour was never able to enjoy the little castle, two of the fireplaces installed at the Petit Trianon came from her residence, the Hôtel d'Evreux, which has since become the Elysée Palace. The King wanted to have his retinue kept to a minimum in his new retreat, and to this end, had "flying" tables made by Loriot. The tables were described by a contemporary: "They rise up from the kitchens, dressed with food, with four other trolley tables, to provide the guests with all the utensils they need, so they can do without subordinates serving them. The tables descend back down through the floor with the same facility." These frequent stays at the Petit Trianon were special moments that the King shared henceforth with Madame du Barry.

Finally, Louis XV undertook the construction of a chapel in 1774, which he did not live to see. He came down with a fever at the Petit Trianon in the spring of 1974. The first surgeon, realizing that the King was gravely ill, advised him to return immediately to the chateau, as a king's death should not occur in such an unofficial setting. Indeed, Louis XV died shortly afterwards, after several days of painful agony.

That same year, Louis XVI made a gift of the Petit Trianon to his wife, Marie-Antoinette. Intended for the new queen's amusement, the small estate was completely remodelled to suit her tastes, under the direction of the architect Mique. A note sent to the Office of the King's Buildings in 1777 ordered: "Everything that has to do with the Petit Trianon must be submitted to Mr. Mique."

The Boudoir of Mobile Mirrors

Marie-Antoinette loved the privacy of small rooms. She created a very clever system of mobile mirrors, which she had installed in this boudoir to cover up the windows.

The Queen had already shown a preference for less classical residences than the Chateau of Versailles, such as Marly, La Muette and the Tuileries, but the Petit Trianon instantly became her sojourn of predilection. The nineteen-year-old sovereign first took an interest in the gardens, which she had rearranged into an English park, making few changes in the building, except to have a boudoir installed, which still retains the décor she chose for it, and renovating a few rooms.

The fashion under Louis XVI was picturesque. Le Nôtre's garden designs seem remote indeed from those sketched out under the influence of pre-romanticism. The era of the gardener's line and the long vista was over, replaced by carefully but discreetly orchestrated disorder and shady, sinuous paths, perfect for strolling (Rousseau composed his *Rêveries d'un promeneur solitaire* in 1776). Ornamental pools and fountains gave way to lakes where the Queen had rocks placed or islands created for effect. Every sort of artifice was used to imitate nature, which had long been domesticated at Versailles.

Chinoiseries, favored in furniture since the time of Louis XV, now invaded the gardens in the form of small, rugged towers. Scattered among the groves were grottos and moss-covered artificial ruins. Marie-Antoinette set about adapting the gardens to the new Anglo-Chinese fashion as soon as she became the mistress of the Petit Trianon.

The Comte de Caraman, a frequent guest at the Court, had already designed similar properties for her in Paris and Roissy, which inspired Mique who, along with the landscape artist Hubert Robert, was placed in charge of the metamorphosis. Steeped in antiquity, which was in vogue at the time, Hubert Robert had visited Italy a few years earlier and brought back sketches of a bucolic countryside, which he materialized in his work here.

The rare essences in the botanical gardens of Louis XV were transported to Paris, and in their place appeared grassy meadows, punctuated with two lakes joined by a meandering river. Jussieu completed the landscape by planting tall trees, and small buildings gradually studded the estate.

The Belvedere, also known as the Music Room, was built behind the Petit Trianon in 1777, on a little island in the center of the Small Lake. It was reached by a wooden footbridge, suspended from a rocky wall, amid a tangle of vegetation. The simple, octagonal pavilion,

Main façade of the Petit Trianon

Gabriel built this delightful little square castle from 1763 to 1768. He added the rich decoration of four huge Corinthian columns to the rear façade giving onto the French-style garden.

Twelve white columns surmounted by a cupola surround a statue of Cupid fashioning himself a bow from Hercules' club, sculpted by Bouchardon. The Queen could enjoy this sight from the windows of her bedchamber at the Petit Trianon.

Imagination was encouraged at the Petit Trianon and the festivities that took place there offered an occasion to adorn the gardens with tents and trellis archways, through which the guests moved about seated on donkeys, to the sound of musicians. This taste for outdoor celebrations was reminiscent of Louis XIV a hundred years earlier, with less solemnity but the same love of stage settings. As often as she could, Marie-Antoinette withdrew here to engage in amusements, surrounded by a few friends of her own age, free from the obligations of Court etiquette. The Billiard Room and Music Room were the scene of joyful, relaxed entertainment, which her chambermaid, Madame Campan, described in her memoirs: "The Queen was no longer the queen at Trianon; she was barely the mistress of the house," the Goncourt brothers reported.

The turbulent young Queen particularly enjoyed music. She had her own box at the Paris Opera, which she regularly attended. She was not inclined to be a mere spectator, however. She played the harpsichord and the harp, and also liked to sing under the direction of the composer Piccinni or Gluck, who had once been her teacher in Vienna. Finally, to satisfy her taste for theatre, she ordered Mique to build a theatre, which was completed in 1780. Like Madame de Pompadour before her, Marie-Antoinette willingly took part in performances given before a small audience of friends and family. She played the role of Rosine in *The Barber of Seville* in the little theatre with its blue and gold décor.

Beaumarchais had *The Marriage of Figaro* performed here for the first time, which today seems to conceal signs of imminent change in the order of things. The play, considered "unforgettable" by Louis XVI, was in fact forbidden and the author (formerly the music teacher of the daughters of Louis XV) was even imprisoned for a time.

The public was rarely admitted at the Trianon, and contrary to custom, the Queen disappeared

Interior of the Belvedere

Octogonal on the outside, circular on the inside, the Music Room, also known as the Stone Room, features the special charm of small-proportioned constructions. One can easily conjure up the delightful picture of the young Queen, surrounded by a few very close friends in this airy décor. The edifice is vaguely reminiscent of the bandstands so dear to the Viennese.

flanked by eight sphinxes, testifies to the extraordinary grace Mique gave to his creations.

If one walks up a few steps, one can see the floor inside, covered with a mosaic of pale, colored marble, adding a special charm to the room, which opens out onto the gardens through eights sets of French doors.

The next year Mique installed the Temple of Love on another island, formed by two arms of the river.

whenever strollers arrived in the vicinity. Her desire to escape from the public gaze drove her to have a special system of mirrors installed which she could move to cover the windows of her boudoir. Never had a sovereign hidden herself away to this extent and she was bitterly reproached for her desire to live, not as a queen, but as a wealthy woman in her own home. The area drew many visitors after the Revolution, mostly curiosity-seekers looking for remains of the past. The nostalgic were not the only ones to appreciate the place, and one clever merchant took unexpected advantage of it.

The boudoir of Marie-Antoinette was transformed into a restaurant, the rooms of the little palace were rented out at exorbitant prices and vendors invaded the gardens. The innkeeper stayed in business until 1805, when Napoleon was thinking of offering the Petit Trianon to his sister, Pauline.

The Empress Eugénie, who liked to surround herself with souvenirs of the Queen at all of her residences, filled the Petit Trianon with objects that had once belonged to Marie-Antoinette.

Le Belvedere

The autumn season is particularly enhanced by the jigsaw style of the Anglo-Chinese gardens. Such gardens were in vogue at the end of the 18th century, when architects and landscape designers altered nature so as to create views of rocks or a hillock or a lake at every bend in the path.

The Hamlet

In 1783, twelve small houses inspired by Norman farmhouses were built along the shores of the Grand Lake. The white half-timbered walls covered with ivy and roses, thatched roofing and wooden galleries were reflected in the lake, dotted with water lilies. The miniature village, nestled among the foliage, seems to belong to a fairy tale rather than to a royal estate.

The Hamlet was intended as a place for pleasure, although, at least at the time of construction, it had real farmers, cowherds and fieldworkers. The houses were surrounded by kitchen gardens and herds grazed along the paths. Only one of the two original dairies remains. A dovecote, a "fishery," a barn used as a ballroom, a linen house and a mill, completed the décor. Marie-Antoinette did not "dress up and play peasant" as some caricatures have suggested, but she did prefer this environment to all the marble of the chateau. She often came here with her children. The fishery was named the "Tower of Marlborough," after a song the Dauphin's nanny used to hum.

On the first floor of the long house, the Queen reserved three rooms for herself with luxurious furnishings in sharp contrast to the rustic exterior. Her private domain also included a "billiard room," a boudoir, a game room, a dining room, a salon and a dressing room, all of them located in the two main buildings.

In October 1789, the Queen was at the Hamlet when a page came galloping over to warn her that a crowd of Parisians was on its way to the chateau.

The setting, straight out of an operetta, always enchants visitors. In the early 20th century, some claimed to have seen "young girls wearing white kerchiefs tucked into their dresses," young men with shoe buckles dating from the time of the kings, and even Marie-Antoinette herself, sketching under a wide-brimmed straw hat. Oddly enough, only English and American visitors ever reported such "visions."

The Queen's House

This thatch-covered house, with its slightly sloping roof, is the main construction among the twelve that originally made up the Hamlet. It is one of the archetypal popular images associated with Marie-Antoinette.

Page 112
Versailles in the fields

Despite their rustic look and the animals encountered in the immediate vicinity, the little houses where the Queen liked to relax, all had very stylish salons. Some of the houses were set aside for the cowherds and gardeners who lived in the Hamlet.

Versailles vers 1688.
Vue des étangs de la butte de Montboron.

Veue du Chasteau et J

rdin de Versailles.

Painted by W. Miller.

THE MEMORABLE ADDRESS of ~ Lewis th

After his Counsel M. Deséze had C

120

Sixteenth AT THE BAR OF THE NATIONAL CONVENTION

l his Defence on the 26 of December 1792

125

PETIT TRIANON

TAPIS VERT

TRIANON

PETIT TRIANON

SAVIGNY-S.-ORGE

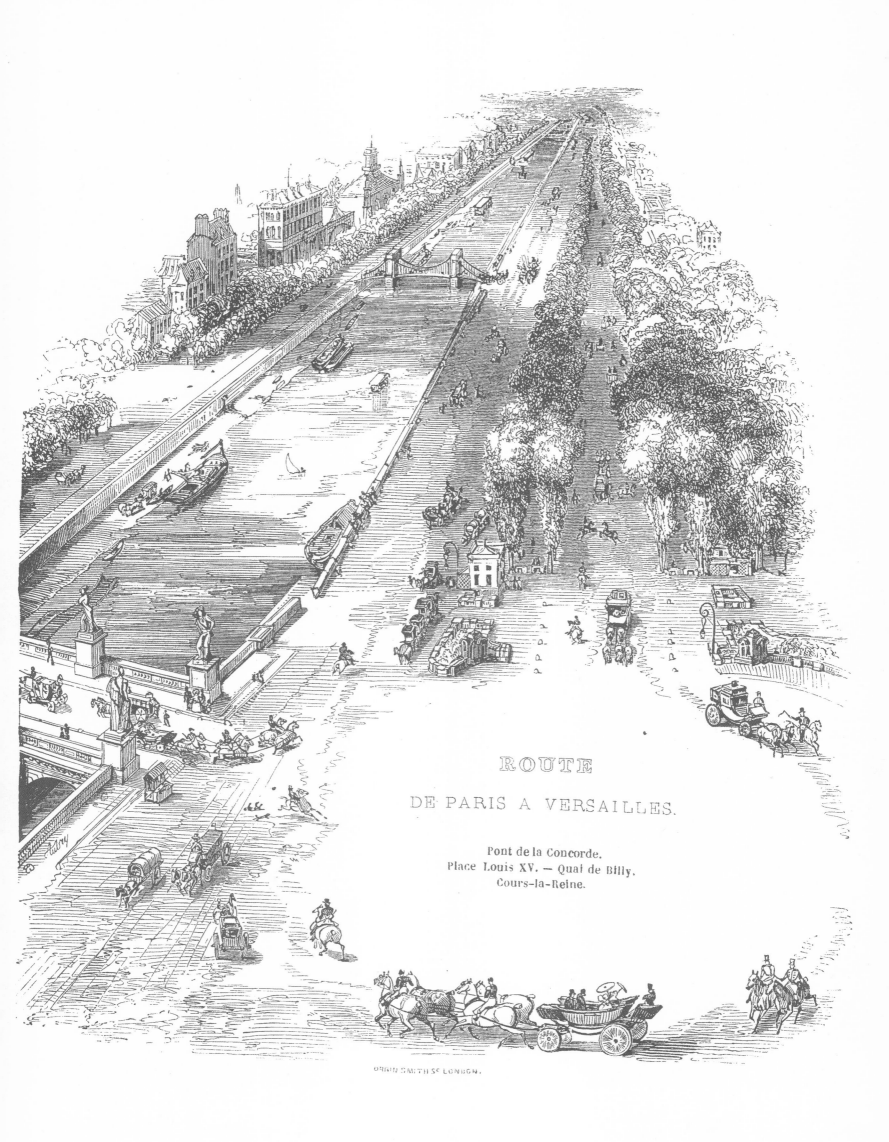

ROUTE

DE PARIS A VERSAILLES.

Pont de la Concorde.
Place Louis XV. — Quai de Billy.
Cours-la-Reine.

PLAN DU PRÈMIER ETAGE ET DES APARTEMANS DU CHATEAU ROYAL DE VERSAILLES.

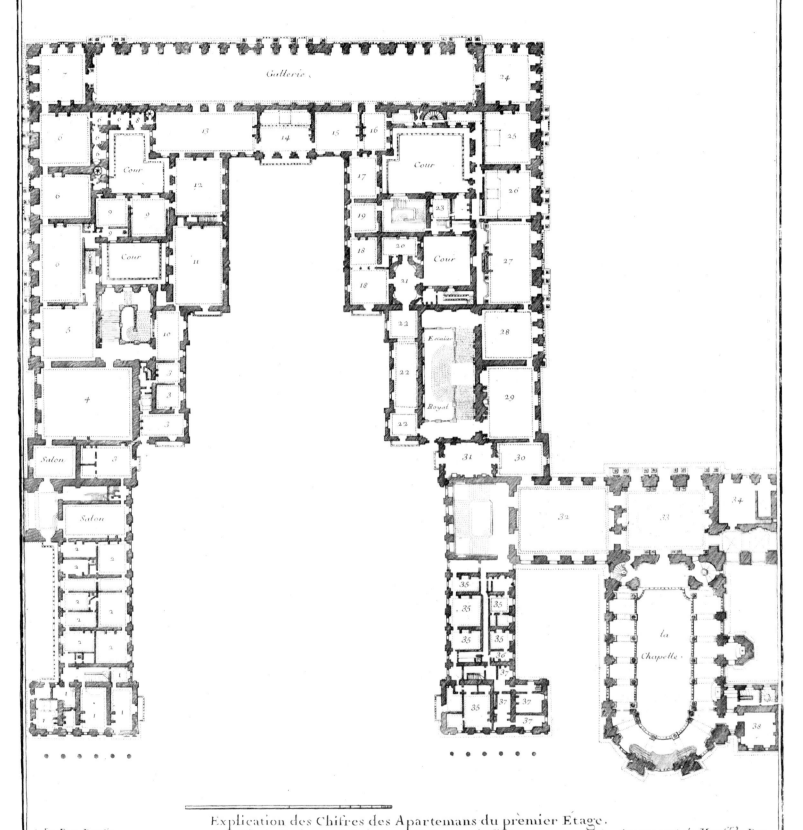

Gallerie

Cour · Cour · Cour · Cour

Salon · Salon · Salon

Escalier Royal

la Chapelle

Explication des Chifres des Apartemans du prèmier Etage.

1. Le Duc Danfin.
2. Apartemans des Enfans de France.
3. Apartemant de Mad.le de Maintenon.
4. Grande Salle des Gardes.
5. Salle des Gardes de la Reine.
6. Apartemant de la Reine.
7. Salon de la Paix.
8. Apartemant du premier Valet de chambre.
9. Apartemant de Monf.r le Daufin Bourgogne.
10. Salon de l'Escalier de la Reine.

11. Salle des Gardes pour le Roi.
12. Chambre ou le Roi mange.
13. Antichambre du Roi.
14. Chambre du Roi.
15. Chambre du Conseil.
16. Cabinet des Peruques.
17. Chambre des Chiens du Roi.
18. Cabinets des Agates et Bijoux.
19. Salon du petit Escalier du Roi.
20. Cabinets des Livres du Roi.
21. Salon de l'Ovale.
22. Petite Gallerie du Roi.

23. Garçons du Chateau.
24. Salon de la Guerre.
25. Chambre du Trône.
26. Chambre du Lit.
27. Salle du Bal.
28. Chambre du Billard.
29. Grande Salle de l'Escalier du Roi.
30. Petit Salon du Cabinet.
31. Cabinet des Medailles et Bijoux.
32. Grand Salon.
33. Salon de la Chapelle.

34. Apartemant de Monf.r le Duc de Chartres.
35. Logement du Gouverneur.
36. Logement du Concierge.
37. Logem.t du Confesseur du Roi.
38. Salle de la Musique du Roi.

A Paris chez De Morlin sur le Pont Notre Dame. Avec Privilege du Roi.

16